HUMOR IN PASCAL

AN EXAMINATION OF THE COMIC HUMOR
OF THE FRENCH PHILOSOPHER PASCAL

By

OLGA WESTER RUSSELL

THE CHRISTOPHER PUBLISHING HOUSE
NORTH QUINCY, MASSACHUSETTS

PRINTED IN

THE UNITED STATES OF AMERICA

#2867341

HUMOR IN PASCAL

*To my Mother, whose very nature was religious,
and to my Father, who was goodness itself,
both of whom loved music and laughter.*

HUMOR IN PASCAL

Contents

Part One

Humor in the *Provinciales*

The First *Provinciale*
The Comedy of Errors:
Mistaken Identities

The *Provinciales* have been examined from many points of view, of meaning, of composition, of style, of sources; let us consider them from one viewpoint: what it is that produces their comic effect and what is the large range of tones of humor which are frequently referred to in general terms. A study in detail of the first letter may reveal what techniques of comedy set the tone at least for the earlier letters before the change to violent vituperation in the later ones.

The letter is true comedy, answering to the need for a detached intellectual attitude which is the essence of the comic pose. Montalte, as the letter writer, dominates the recital and he remains objective. He does not become angry, though his opponent, M. N.'s brother-in-law, may lose his composure. Even the suggestion of a serious message at the end of the letter takes the form of a quip.

The pace is rapid, with a comedian's sense of timing, the effect achieved by a condensed interlacing of techniques of tone, gesture, language, attitude, situation, composition, and character.

It is interesting that Bergson, in *le Rire*, considers comedy only in terms of the theater. Yet Pascal is dramatic in prose,[1] as is La Fontaine in poetry, and the same

1. Note the source indicated for arguments, plan, and initial idea, "un

terms apply. Interesting, too, that Bergson's definition of distraction, absentmindedness, lack of suppleness, mechanization applied to human nature, as the springboard for comic effect finds constant application here. As in the theater, almost the whole of this lively letter is direct conversation, and the rest is in epistolary form, an extension of conversation, requiring little more space than would scenic directions, or prologue and epilogue.

Comedy of character. Marionettes. Who holds the strings?

The characters are few, as in classical comedy: Montalte; M. N., ardently against the Jansenists; his brother-in-law, a Jansenist "if ever there was one"; the Molinist, disciple of M. Le Moine; and the Jacobin (the Dominican). All are comic. They are types and, except for Montalte, have little to distinguish them aside from their professional distortion, so that it is difficult to remember which one is being interviewed. The last three are even a multiplication of one type, with slight variation, such a group as one finds in *les Femmes savantes* or *les Précieuses ridicules*, the repetition tending to heighten the ridicule, since it is by surface traits that we note comic resemblance.[2] Nature should not repeat itself or turn out types like a machine.

---

grand nombre d'arguments, le plan de sa discussion et aussi l'idée première de la scène comique qu'il imagine" in *Défense de la Proposition de Mr Arnauld Docteur de Sorbonne, touchant le droit*, attributed to Nicole, which appeared shortly after a letter of M . Chamillard of December 11, 1655—Pascal, *Oeuvres completes*, ed. L. Brunschvig, P. Boutroux, and F. Gazier, Les Grands Ecrivains de la France, vol. IV (Paris: Hachette, 1914), p. 112. These elements are richly added to by Pascal.

2. Pascal notes it: "Deux visages semblables, dont aucun ne fait rire en particulier font rire ensemble par leur ressemblance"—No. 13 of the *Pensées*, in *Oeuvres complètes*, l'Intégrale (Paris: Seuil, 1963). Further references will be to this edition.

Montalte is a multiplication in himself of recognizable and established comic roles. We see him as intelligent and clear-minded, but at the same time naïvely observing and easily surprised, and in that humorous. He assumes the guise of a Candide ("Tant d'assemblées d'une compagnie aussi célèbre qu'est la Faculté de Paris"), wishing to give the appearance of being carried away by his admiration for the learned men of the Sorbonne and apparently willing to consider seriously, as it is offered on the surface, all that is said to him. In that, he is a literary convention, like Candide, a one-dimensional character, with the added interest here of the comic value of disguise, of the artificial plastered over the natural.

This is a combination of no little importance for he will use his disguise as a *dupeur*, a manipulator of his opponents, thereby taking on another specialized comic dimension. Clever, astute, he delights in maneuvering his adversaries with the deftness of Beaumarchais' Figaro: "Pour en être mieux reçu, je feignis d'être fort des siens." Montalte, then, represents the public, in the good bourgeois tradition, taking his revenge upon the clerics who would confuse him to preserve their own power. At the same time, his adversaries are his puppets; when he succeeds in stirring one to the disadvantage of anger, he notes with glee: "*Mon* homme s'échauffa là-dessus." Moreover, he is not above maneuvering the reader, the public, for he disarms them by adding "mais d'un zèle dévot" so that no one can say he is cruel to a good man.

As did Henri Bergson, *Oeuvres* (Paris: Presses Universitaires de France, 1959), p. 403.

Note, too, that Pascal classes this thought under *Vanité*. Bergson finds vanity to be the hallmark of the comic character, rather than egotism, vanity being a more surface characteristic and therefore more correctable by laughter (p. 470).

Also, almost throughout, he plays the vaudeville role of "straight man" to the comedian, tossing him his cues, knowing what is coming and where he is leading him. As straight man he asks loaded questions: "Serait-il possible que la Sorbonne introduisit dans l'Eglise cette erreur, que tous les justes ont toujours le pouvoir d'accomplir les commandements?" The word "error" throws his adversary off base, and he gets an answer that has nothing to do with the point: "qu'il ne déguiserait jamais ses sentiments pour quoi que ce fût [no one had spoken of disguising]; que c'était sa créance et que lui et tous les siens la défendraient jusqu'à la mort. . . . " It is like the reader of advertisements who wrote to a cigarette company to ask on what specific tests was based the statement that their cigarette caused less coughs than another, and was answered, "Yes, of course, tests prove that our cigarette. . . . "

Add to that a sense of humor that can see himself as comic. Montalte does, once, take over the role of comedian, caught in his own trap (for the moment *le dupeur dupé*). He asks if his opponent admits *le pouvoir prochain* (proximate power), which is another loaded question, and is asked what he himself means by it. On the defensive, since he does not know, and making fun of himself, he throws out the remark *au hasard* (he is distracted), but nevertheless getting in another word of partisanship to stir up his man: "Je l'entends au sens des Molinistes." Pinned down to *which* Molinist, helpless, he abandons astuteness: "Je les lui offris tous ensemble. . . . " Notwithstanding, he is still the "straight man". The difference between Montalte and his opponents is that, when he is caught, he knows he is ridiculous.

Thus Montalte is sketched as the central character, marked by types. He may be bewildered, but he asks for no sympathy, and we can laugh.

What of the others, who have so little to distinguish them one from the other that only one has an initial for a name, and the others have none? The Jansenist is a brother-in-law (Why? A relative, but not acknowledged as a real relative?). One is a disciple (no ideas of his own). One is a Jacobin, member of a group among the Dominicans, a restricted group to ridicule, carried to its extreme, just as the *Précieuses ridicules* are a provincial imitation of a bourgeois imitation of the *grandes dames* of the aristocratic *salons*.[3] Montalte gave us the word, laughing: "Je les lui offris tous ensemble, comme ne faisant qu'un même corps, et n'agissant que par un même esprit." Puppets, but giving a delightful appearance of life. He may call one "Mon Janséniste", but it was his Jansenist who tripped him up. The Jansenist sees the Molinists as a group, with the group's distortion, ridiculous and contradictory in their group loyalty: "Ils sont si peu dans les mêmes sentiments, qu'ils en ont de tout contraires. Mais étant tous unis dans le dessein de perdre M. Arnauld. . . . "[4] United to destroy M. Arnauld, they will agree to use the term *prochain*, though they do not mean the same thing by it, in order to oppress him with the force of numbers. Otherwise, we see him only by gesture: "He laughed and said coldly. . . . "

M. N. lives near Pascal ("qui demeure près de chez

3. Note of Nicole to the second *Provinciale*: "il ne condamne pas tous les Dominicains . . . mais seulement un certain parti du Couvent de Paris, dont le P. Nicolaï est le Chef, et qui dans ces disputes avoit abandonné les sentiments de son ordre, et s'étoit lié avec les Jésuites pour abolir la doctrine de Saint Thomas"—*Oeuvres*, G. E. ed., IV, p. 177.

4. "L'avocat Antoine Arnauld (1560-1619) se fit connaître par son plaidoyer contre les jésuites. Après l'attentat de Jean Chatel, l'expulsion des jésuites hors de France fut prononcée en 1595. Les jésuites, qui reviendront en France en 1603, ne pardonneront jamais à la famille Arnauld." Exposition, "Deux siècles de Jansénisme à travers les documents du fonds Port-Royal d'Utrecht", Museé de l'Histoire de France, 16 janvier-18 mars 1974.

moi"); Pascal had installed himself opposite the Jesuit College to get out his letters anonymously.[5] This would be a secret laugh to be shared only with the few who knew where he was. M. N. is in better and better health; the Jesuits feel triumphant? He was "healthy enough" to take Montalte to his brother-in-law, the Jansenist; it takes assurance to lead him into the other camp. Driven by professional self-importance, he is delighted if one agrees with him: "Tout beau! il faut être théologien pour en voir le fin." He is cold, rude, if one tries to pin him down: "il me rebuta rudement."

The disciple, "one of the disciples" of M. Le Moine,[6] answers pompously when he can agree to a simple example: "Doctement, me dit-il." When he cannot, he retreats into his discipleship: "Non, me dit-il, suivant M. Le Moine."

In rapid descent, the degree of individuality reaches its lowest point. One Jacobin (Dominican) is addressed separately only once as "mon Père", and gets in only one answer, though it is not clear that only he says it. Otherwise, they are addressed in group and answer as a group, like a Greek chorus ("leur dis-je . . . me dirent-ils"), and they chant together ("tous ensemble"), in Latin, about a term without meaning. They can even be collectively jovial and magnanimous, not seeing where they are being led: "Voilà qui va bien, me répondirent mes Pères en m'embrassant." Do they all crowd around for the gesture? Faced with obvious contradiction in their stand, they say nothing, show no reaction: "Mes Pères ne répondirent rien." *Mes* Pères are manipulated, and not only by their own company. This is the third

5. Ernest Mortimer, *Blaise Pascal, the Life and Work of a Realist* (London: Methuen, 1959), p. 140; Jean Steinmann, *Pascal* (Paris: Descleé de Brouwer, 1962), p. 110.
6. *La Dévotion aisée*, par le jésuite Pierre le Moine, 1652.

person, not direct address; the possessive pronoun becomes slightly ironic, and doubtless a twinkle from Montalte goes with it.

That these characters are capable of false reasoning, of unscrupulously slipping out from under a question[7] ("Attendez . . . vous me pourriez surprendre. Allons tout doucement"), of shifting ground, of taking refuge in pedantry ("*Distinguo*") is obvious and could be serious. What makes this humorous is their unreasonable blindness to their own lack of logic; they are carried away automatically by their aberration, so that they see stubbornness only in their opponent ("Vous êtes opiniâtre") and become arbitrary and childish ("Vous le direz ou vous serez hérétique").

Comedy of situation. Structure. Confrontation and frustration.

The composition of the letter for comedy of situation is as calculated and intellectual as the created, artistic type-characters. The arrangement is classical, a statement of the problem, a certain amount of rapid exposition which amounts to a tirade, a long and lively monologue on Montalte's part, then scenes of successive dialogues, building with crescendo effect to a confrontation with mutual insults, and a conclusion. In part a plan for *le Bourgeois gentilhomme*?

Having indicated by exaggerated terms the storm that rages in the Sorbonne, Montalte states the problem in its simplest essentials: "On examine deux questions, l'une de fait, l'autre de droit." No opportunity for comic effect is lost. The descent from the grandiose to the factual produces the impression of a tempest in a teapot.

His sketching in of the background is in itself dra-

7. Source, in *Oeuvres*, G. E. ed., IV, p. 116: "comme il est ingénieux à trouver des accommodemens."

matic. The present tense places the scene before our eyes. "On propose l'affaire en Sorbonne. Soixante et onze docteurs entreprennent sa défense. . . . " This is not the spirit of considered opinion, but the material weight of numbers to impress upon us that reason can be imposed upon mechanically. We can be distracted and manipulated. These men condemn what they have not seen and do not know exists. Some asked if anyone had seen the propositions in Jansénius; no one had, and some had seen the opposite. On the other hand, eighty doctors, but secular clerics, and forty monks, but those who beg, (greater numbers but of less consequence, to confuse our judgment further) do not want to look at the proposition because truth is not at issue, only the audacity of M. Arnauld. It is a masquerade of professional pomposity, so prone to provoke a laugh. That is not enough; we have fifteen who are indifferent, hardened to social results, isolated in the aim of maintaining their importance. Anticlimax, the ridiculous descent from the largest to the smallest number, and none of them sensible. No one will produce the propositions at issue.

It is like the parade of the Peers in *Iolanthe*, as rollicking as Gilbert and Sullivan in attacking professional privilege, or like the rhythm of the folk song with its medieval flavor, *la Princesse des amours*, who feigns death to get her lover in spite of her father:

> Quarante prêtres, autant d'abbés,
> Suivirent la belle enterreé.

Good sense will have its revenge, which is to laugh. People have to see to believe: "le monde devient méfiant, et ne croit les choses que grand il les voit." One cannot impose upon people with professional show and fanfare.

Thus the question of fact is disposed of by the flashback, in itself a little comedy within the comedy. The

comic pace is maintained, and there is added the delight-
fully magic effect of circles within circles in the structure.
Now to the main forward movement. The question of
grace is at issue, very important.

In the first interview, Montalte, with his ardent
curiosity, stirs the zealous M. N. to rudeness ("il me
rebuta rudement") and to taking refuge in hedging and
obscurity: the opinion is "problématique". Montalte indulges in a hypocritical apology and then irritates him
with an opinion of the Jansenists, urging M. N. to further
abruptness, "You don't understand anything about it"
("Vous n'y entendez rien"), and to more inflated self-
importance, since the learned man states that he upheld
the same thesis himself. Montalte, doubtful and bewildered, asks what the difficulty is and is answered that
M. Arnauld "does not recognize these things the way
we understand them".

There are two comic elements in the situation. Montalte
is pulling the strings, manipulating his opponent to
expose group distortion, professional blindness and
pride. Montalte, also, as he represents the general public,
is in a situation of frustration which will be repeated,
multiplied, aggravated by succeeding scenes. It is man,
who ought to be master of his fate, viewed from outside
in a kind of fumbling helplessness as he tries to find truth
in the face of professional blindness, prejudice, and pride.
Frustration was one of the principal sources of comic
effect for W. C. Fields. It is the action of taking hold of
a doorknob to open a door and having the knob come
off in your hand, or of trying to strike home with a dagger
only to find that the blade is rubber and bends aside
ineffectually. This is not rational or natural. Things in
themselves should not be whimsical. How much more
profound the comic effect if a key that breaks off in a lock
is intellectual, or if the dagger is to puncture the balloon

of professional pomposity and bends against a wall harder than itself, an attitude that the profession, though it be religious, is made for the professional, not for the public.

Montalte goes to the Jansenist and gets him excited into giving contradictory answers to essentially the same question with almost equal fervor. He returns to M. N. to promise accord in the Sorbonne on the strength of a signature in blood. M. N. in unconscious humor asserts that the difference is so esoteric that only a theologian can understand it, and they can hardly notice the difference themselves. But, willfully and childishly, he says that the point at issue is not that but a word, *"prochain"*, *le pouvoir prochain*. Montalte is thrown back into confusion. He confused the Jansenist with words. His weapon is now turned upon himself, with fine boomerang effect. He is the *dupeur dupé*, deceived as he deliberately deceived, as surely as the medieval Pathelin, and not once but many times. At the same time, it is the ludicrous impression of the sort of effort that, constantly renewed, is constantly thrown back with great suddenness to the point of departure, which is confusion. Bergson has seen it as both "reversible" and "circular" movement set up mechanically over against natural movement which should be forward.[8] Frustration is heightened by repetition and by a multiplication of laugh-provoking techniques in each little incident.

The jack-in-the-box effect of putting down one's opponent only to have him bob up again is even more evident when Montalte scurries back to his Jansenist ("je fus promptement retrouver mon Janséniste"), who parries question for question as Montalte, who appears

8. Bergson, *Oeuvres*, pp. 426-427. Bergson remarks that Herbert Spencer and Kant have also noted the laugh provoked by what he calls circular movement and what we have designated as frustration.

to be helplessly laughing at himself, gets apparently
careless and general. Asked if he admits *le pouvoir
prochain*, the Jansenist answers: "Tell me what meaning
you give it and then *I* will tell you what I think about
it." This is a child's answer when he does not know what
to say, as well as the *dupé* trying to dupe the *dupeur*.
Yet with each repetition, as the Jansenist springs back
to the attack, the plot thickens. He indicates that the
Molinists unite in apparent conformity in order to
"oppress with assurance". Montalte, the "innocent",
does not want to believe in their "evil designs". He goes
on ("je fus chez un des disciples") to confound the
characterless disciple with concrete examples. The
choir of Jacobins (Dominicans) in their turn irritate him
into rational indignation: "It is playing with words to use
the same terms when you give them opposite meanings."

The moment of tension is dissipated by the remarkably
opportune arrival of "my disciple of M. Le Moine" ("par
un bonheur qui me parut extraordinaire"). The confrontation is hilarious. Heresy depends upon what terms one
uses, even if one does not use the terms ("Il ne l'appelle
. . . ni prochain, ni non prochain"). The Jacobins
(Dominicans) all nod assent before they are asked, which
inspires no confidence ("Je ne les pris pas pour juges").
One of the bobbing chorus tries to give a definition but
is immediately cut off by the Molinist, who says they
have all agreed not to explain the word *prochain*. Then
everybody fights. Montalte taxes them with chicanery,
with promoting lip-service, and with teaching without
authority from the Church, the Councils, or the Popes.
The Fathers say he is obstinate, and he had better say
what he is told to say, or he will be a heretic along with
M. Arnauld.

In conclusion, Montalte sums up the questions of grace,
which are not condemned at all, and the question of the

word *prochain*, which has clearly not been resolved:
the word has no meaning and should be banished. Since
the whole turns on a word, we come easily to the consideration of the comedy of tone and language.

Comedy of tone. Language. Mock-heroic confusion.

The use of comedy of tone is highly artistic, even to
setting a frame of mock nobility, of heroic elevation, at
the beginning and the end, and ranging in between
through straight-faced ridicule, various transpositions
of tone, irony, a play on words, suggestions of the rhythm
of folk songs. That he ends with a pun, as the form for one
of his most serious thoughts, gives evidence of sustained
comic attitude and should convince us that we can have
fun with Pascal, as he had fun with this letter.[9]

He opens with ironic hyperbole to show what ought to
be, considering the dignity of the Sorbonne, [10] and what
is not. The poetic suggestion of vastness in the plurals
("Tant d'assemblées . . . choses . . . extraordinaires")
is curiously intermingled with the informal exclamatory
terms ("si", "aussi", "tant", "bien", "extraordinaire") into
which a letter writer can fall easily and which call to
mind the effusions of ladies in a salon (*les Femmes
savantes*). It is the tone on two levels that creates the
comic irony and diminishes the importance of the issue
to sheer frivolity: "tant de choses si extraordinaires, et
si hors d'exemple, en font concevoir une si haute idée,
qu'on ne peut croire qu'il n'y en ait un sujet bien extraordinaire." Yet inversely, the very repetition of the

9. "le calembour fut supprimé dans les éditions ultérieures"—Pascal,
Les Provinciales, ed. Steinmann (Paris: Colin, 1962), p. 280; but the
suppressions were not Pascal's (p. 11 of this edition).
10. Source in the *Défense*, attributed to Nicole: "Qui pourroit croire
qu'on excitast de si grands troubles dans l'Eglise pour un sujet si
ridicule? . . . qu'on occupast si longtemps la plus célèbre Faculté du
monde . . . "—*Oeuvres*, G. E. ed., IV, p. 118.

expressions of elevated importance does create the attitude of awe and respect which are a part of the assumed character of Montalte. After such brilliance ("un si grand éclat"), the simple factual statement of the problem, set off in a paragraph by itself ("On examine deux questions: l'une de fait, l'autre de droit"), produces such an abrupt descent that it takes the wind out of one's sails. The transposition of tone pricks the balloon of pomposity.

The end of the letter resumes on an even higher level of oratorical bombast, applied to the word *prochain*: "Happy the peoples who never heard of it! Happy the generations that preceded its birth!" Let the Academy banish this barbarous word which threatens to under-mine the dignity of the Sorbonne. With the mock heroic tone, Pascal puts his neat, artistic, artificial frame (as though life could be put in a frame) around a comic epic —so flimsy a pretext for dispute in a dignified body ("indigne de la Sorbonne et de la théologie")—a satire worthy of Boileau in *le Lutrin*.

The language reflects repeatedly this abrupt ironical descent from the sublime to the ridiculous: "Soixante et onze . . . quatre vingts docteurs . . . quinze . . . indifférents." Montalte became a "great" theologian in very "little" time, which makes the argument simple when it should be profound. He is edified ("bien glor-ieux") to know the real point ("le noeud de l'affaire"), at which point he finds himself thoroughly unen-lightened. A concluding paragraph speaks of this "solid" reasoning about a word with no meaning at all.

There is the detached comic language that looks down upon the actions of the puppets and invites the reader to enjoy the same feeling of superiority: "odd" that they will not produce the disputed proposition ("le refus bizarre qu'on fait de les montrer"). Baudelaire finds the sense of superiority to be the dominating idea in laughter.[11]

One notes the comedy of tone that suggests gesture or expression of physiognomy and, in doing so, isolates the gesture from the essence of the person so that one sees him effectively from the outside, and so, as comic: "Il me rebuta rudement", of the indignant M. N.; "Voilà qui va bien", reinforced by its repetition, evoking the beaming countenances, identically reproduced, of the Jacobin Fathers. The Jansenist, not wanting to be caught in a statement, "began to laugh and said coldly" ("se mit à rire et me dit froidement"), as he threw the disputed term back at the speaker in order to put him on the defensive.

Professional jargon is essentially comic, a dead giveaway, when it takes over the speaker so that he is unwittingly hypocritical: in his hedging language ("cette opinion est problématique"); in hiding behind Latin to gain time ("distinguo"); in using the word *prochain* divorced of all meaning, "Have we not agreed to say it, without saying what it means?" ("Ne sommes-nous pas demeurés d'accord . . . ?") Deliberate obscurity in language goes one step further, and Montalte protests the term "prochain": "I think that it was invented only to confuse." He commits it to memory because it has nothing to do with his intelligence.

A reversal of terms, one word set into a sentence that should go straight along, reversing and upsetting its direction, forces a laugh: M. N. takes Montalte to his brother-in-law, who is a Jansenist, if ever there was one, and yet a good fellow ("et pourtant fort bon homme").

---

11. Charles Baudelaire, *De l'essence du rire et généralement du comique dans les arts plastiques, Oeuvres complètes*, Bibliothèque de la Pléiade (Paris: Gallimard, 1961), p. 980: "Le rire vient de l'idée de sa propre supériorité."

The one word "pourtant" marks the prejudice of the Jesuit. Tolstoy, in *War and Peace*, uses the word with equal effect to show professional blindness, ignorance, a self-serving profession: when Pierre, ill, was taken to the city, the doctors gave him medicine and drugs; "nevertheless", he got better.

A crescendo of emotional phrases which carries a speaker away, away from his point, becomes ludicrous: "Mon homme s'échauffa", but with pious zeal, and said he would not disguise his sentiments for anyone; "that that was his belief, that he and all his people would defend it to the death. . . . " Anything stated so "seriously" would have to be believed, maintains Montalte ironically. Montalte is not carried away.

Ingenuous language that takes the meaning out of what it says would delight any child or grown-up. Thus, M. N.'s magnanimous statement: "One has to be a theologian to see the point. The difference there is between us is so subtle that we can hardly see it ourselves; it would be too difficult for you to understand."

One or two words effect comic diminution. Montalte offered the Molinists "all together" ("Je les lui offris tous ensemble"), as though one could pick people up as a group and hand them over. A word that transposes to a familiar tone in a serious discussion will destroy dignity equally well, as for the poor Jacobin, momentarily separated from his group, but not far, by exasperation: "*Oui-da*, he would be according to us, if he is not blind."

An effective repetition of a phrase is funny when it underlines the beaming agreement of the Dominican Fathers: "Voilà qui va bien." It is funnier when Montalte repeats the phrase exactly again to turn their contradictions back upon them.

The direct invective of satire appears briefly, as a

foretaste of what will come later: "It is playing on words, to say you agree because you use common terms, when you do not agree on the meanings." The effect of attack is immediately lightened by the suggested deadpan lack of response, in the ironical "Mes Pères ne répondirent rien", and by the fortuitous arrival of the disciple of M. Le Moine. Montalte taxes them indignantly with chicanery and equivocation ("une pure chicanerie . . . d'user de mots équivoques et captieux"). At the same time, the insistence on the material form of the word ("il faut prononcer les syllabes *pro, chain*") with no relation to its meaning is comic in itself, heavy with the labored exasperation of the speaker. Once again Montalte sums up: "One must say it with the lips, for fear of being heretical in name." This tension, too, is relieved by the delightful negation of all authority but their own and their turning on Montalte the epithet of "obstinate" ("opiniâtre").

Equally consistent is the arbitrary, childish tone of the seventy-one, or eighty, and fifteen learned doctors who paraded before us in the beginning and whose exit line is like a chant: "You will say it or you will be a heretic and M. Arnauld, too. For we are the greatest number, and if we have to, we'll bring in so many Franciscans that we'll carry the day." Their recessional is accompanied by the music of mock-heroic exhortation: "Heureux les peuples . . . ! heureux ceux qui . . . !"

Montalte has his own little aside for the reader: he leaves him the liberty of holding out for the word *prochain* or not, for he loves his *prochain* too much to persecute him on that score. The play on words, typically untranslatable, provokes the laugh. The exchange of charity for prejudice is wittily implied. As his true and deepest conclusion, it will carry the writer into the *Pensées*. Here it is expressed lightly, pleasurably.

To make sure the reader goes out smiling, he has one more line: "If this story does not displease you, I will keep you informed of all that goes on." What is this rhythm:

> Si ce récit ne vous déplaît pas,
> je continuerai de vous avertir
> de tout ce qui se passera.?

Is it the closing stanza of the little song, "Il était un petit navire"?

> Si cette histoire vous amuse,
> Si cette histoire vous amuse,
> Nous allons la, la, la recommencer.
> Nous allons la, la, la recommencer.

The Second *Provinciale*
Assorted Adversaries

It seems difficult from the beginning to group the letters according to tone or comic approach, so gradually and yet rapidly does the balance and stance change. All the seeds of what is to come are in the first letter. In the second the balance shifts both for character and arrangement of presentation. There are much more developed and sustained speeches by a Jansenist presenting a social approach, such as one gets from Philinthe in *le Misanthrope*. The direction becomes more obviously defined as attacking what Mr. Carnochan has called, in speaking of another satirist, false nobility, pious unconcern, the hypocrisy of power.[1]

Bergson draws an exceedingly subtle distinction between wit and humor[2] and between irony and humor, both of which he declares to be elements of satire.[3] This would seem to narrow the definition of humor unnecessarily. There is after all a fine line between a smile and a laugh; what makes one person smile will make another laugh. Baudelaire takes his examples of caricature (and even of pantomime in the theater[4]) over a wider geo-

1. W. B. Carnochan, "Juvenal as a Satirist," *PMLA* (March, 1970).
2. "L'esprit . . . du comique volatilisé"—Bergson, *Oeuvres*, p. 439.
3. Bergson, *Oeuvres*, p. 448.
4. The English Pierrot on the French stage—*De l'essence du rire*, pp. 988-990.

graphical area (England, Germany, Spain, Italy, Holland)[5], thus fulfilling Bergson's own specification that comedy springs from an "observation extérieure"[6], and Baudelaire comes up with other sources of laughter. What he calls "le comique significatif", which runs parallel with Bergson's definition of comedy as correctional, for social utility, when pushed to its limits becomes "le comique féroce".[7] Laughter bites, says Baudelaire ("l'homme mord avec le rire"[8]). Baudelaire goes deep and finds wide horizons: laughter, being the result of man's contradictory double nature, becomes the perpetual explosion of his anger and his suffering.[9] Thus a caricature can be heavy with bile and rancor.[10] M. Guillemin, treating the wide range of Hugo's humor, considers that in epigrams and satire laughter becomes slightly deformed, but he claims validity for the humor of combat: "si l'humour noir et l'humour leste sont des genres classés, l'humour 'rosse', l'humour de combat ont aussi leur tradition."[11] For Mr. Weber, "laughter, satire, and irony are of the same stuff".[12]

Structure.   Take aim and fire in all directions.

The structure of the second letter is in the main very much simplified, allowing for sustained discussion of ideas. There is not so much running about. A rather

5. Baudelaire, *Quelques Caricaturistes étrangers, Oeuvres*, pp. 1014-1024, & *De l'essence du rire*, pp. 987-988.
6. Bergson, *Oeuvres*, p. 468.
7. *De l'essence du rire*, p. 987.
8. *Ibid.*, p. 978.
9. *Ibid.*, p. 981.
10. *Ibid.*, p. 979.
11. Henri Guillemin, *L'Humour de Victor Hugo* (Neuchatel: Ed. de la Baconnière, 1951), p. 65.
12. Joseph Gardner Weber, "The Persuasive Art of Pascal's *Lettres Provinciales*: a Study of Satire, Irony and Argumentation" (Ph.D. diss., Illinois University, 1963), p. 12.

lengthy conversation between M. N. and Montalte sets
up briefly the difference between the Jesuits, the Jansenists, and the Dominicans on the question of grace,
and a longer explanation of the Dominicans' stand and
the strategy of the Jesuits in uniting with them. The
main scene, a very long one, takes place between a
Jansenist, who dominates it, a Dominican, and Montalte.
The very brief epilogue by Montalte is no more than
a summing up in a play on words, and a practical transition to other letters. This trimmed-down construction
seems to have one comic aim, to take a joyous time out
to shoot down the weaker opponent and thus clear the
field and narrow the problem to a zestful attack on the
stronger and essential adversary. There is the slight
complication first of a clash between Montalte and the
Dominican, then between the Jansenist and the Dominican, and finally Montalte, who eggs them all on, cannot
resist taking the Jansenist down off his pinnacle a little,
too. There remains the comic, childish, fabricated delight of the play within the play, the fine little farce
disguised as a parable, to break up the rhythm of the
long presentation of the Jansenist, which might otherwise become too tedious a tirade.

Characters.   The Dominican center stage.

There are only four main characters, and they begin
to emerge a little more definitely. As comic characters
they are still sketched with the briefest lines. M. N.
remains half disguised. His role is to introduce, to
explain, and to lead to the main scene. He is a strategist
("Il sait parfaitement le secret des Jésuites"), and he is
always with the Jesuits and with their leaders. He has
his own strings to pull; he asserts that the Jesuits are
not the greater dupes in the situation ("la suite fera voir
que ces derniers ne sont pas les plus dupes"). He re-

mains apparently detached; the Jesuits are always spoken of in the third person, like the others. He does not come clear as the villain in melodrama, but he is profoundly disabused; he has no admiration for the "friends" of the Jesuits, with their ambiguous stand. He is an "honest" scoundrel: the end justifies the means, in union for power. Why fight the Dominicans? What poor political strategy! ("Il faut ménager davantage ceux qui sont puissants dans l'Eglise.") He has as little admiration for the general public, for the world is well paid with words ("le monde se paye de paroles: peu approfondissent les choses . . . ").

Yet he remains unconscious in his own aberrations and seems unaware of the flimsiness of his pretense. Hypocrisy has so taken hold of him that he is not his own master, and he does not know it. He can say with a straight face: Ask the Dominicans to say that their statements are illogical? "That would be pressing them too much. You cannot tyrannize over your friends!" Over your enemies, yes, is the implication. But the enemy to such a character is only one he thinks he can manage to safely dispose of. Like the Jesuits, he is complacent in his reasoning. Practical necessity justifies the strategy. The Dominicans have offered too many obstacles in history. Let them say one thing and mean another as long as they join with us. The Jesuits "sont bien satisfaits de leur complaisance".

He knows what he is doing and his ideas are clear. To the Jesuit, sufficient grace means man has enough and has the free will to act on it or not. The Jansenist says there is no sufficient grace unless it is acted on; only God can give efficacious grace. The Dominicans doctrine is "bizarre": they agree that all men have sufficient grace, but they need God to bestow efficacious grace, and that is not granted to all.

Montalte leaves M. N. the center of the stage for the moment, content to have him expose himself. Montalte pursues his former tactics just enough to spur the discussion on. Ask the right question with seeming ingenuity. Offer enough objection to expose agreement to the contradiction: "the Dominicans say the term without thinking it." They join with the Jesuits in a word that has no meaning and agree with the Jansenists in substance. And M. N. answers, "Cela est vrai", for both Montalte and he hold themselves apparently apart from the poor Dominican, the victim of the next scene. Neither Montalte nor M. N. cares how far the Dominicans lose face, as long as the Jesuits can count them in their numbers.

When Montalte sees the Dominican sufficiently demolished, he will pin him down "gently" to his inconsistency: "How can you apply the term sufficient to a grace which is insufficient in fact?" When the Dominican in answer pleads solely the motive of ambition ("notre crédit"), Montalte, seeing him speak so sadly, says that he pities him. But this is a pity which carries suspicious overtones of conscious superiority and has achieved the calculated aim of laying bare spiritual poverty and weakness where integrity should be expected. This pity and gentleness can also partly disarm the reader who can even laugh at himself, knowing the game.

For the moment all these characters and the reader, too, join together like the animals in the *Roman de Renart* in the gaiety of true Gallic wit. No one is better than anyone else. We all go around deceiving each other and ourselves. Montalte knows when a moment of *détente* is necessary. Bergson calls it a temporary distraction of the will, a relief from the intellectual tension of common sense.[13] Baudelaire finds a more profound reason for

13. Bergson, *Oeuvres*, pp. 480 & 481.

giving in to laughter. Man can save himself even through the signs of his weakness: "avec le rire il adoucit quelquefois son coeur et l'attire; car les phénomènes engendrés par la chute deviendront les moyens du rachat."[14] But is not the relaxation really a recognition of common humanity? Can we not be glad for a moment to see others as full of foibles as ourselves? Is there not a sense of fellowship which means that we do not really have a high opinion of ourselves and would like for an instant not to have to put on the appearance of virtue, a good face on things, the common social mask that we use even against ourselves?

No one will let us do it very long. Montalte can take a back seat for a moment and use the Jansenist ("mon ami, plus sérieux que moi") to pull the situation into line. We all have the austerity of our own Jansenist in us to set our common sense to working.

Montalte has conceded that the Jesuits are clever, a safe enough statement for our diplomatic master of ceremonies, and he proceeds to the Jacobin camp.[15] A Jansenist happens to be at the door looking for someone else.[16] The writer of comedy does not bother himself about fortuitous entrances, as witness an official appearing in the *dénouement* of a Molière comedy to announce a reversal of fortunes (*le Tartuffe*).[17]

14. *De l'essence du rire*, p. 978.

15. It is always useful to remember that Jacobin=Dominican=Thomist.

16. How much more comical than the suggestion in the possible sources: "Supposons donc qu'un de ces pretendus Heterodoxes qui ne veulent pas avoüer ce pouvoir prochain . . . aille trouver M. le Moine [Nicole imitates *le P.* Gaborens, *Discours d'un Religieux*, Paris, 1652] . . . mais que retenant toujours une secrete aversion pour le Molinisme, il prie le P. Nicolaï d'assister à la conférence . . . " —*Oeuvres*, G. E. ed., IV, p. 115.

17. Though Ms. Zwillenberg finds greater comic significance in this ending. Myrna Kogan Zwillenberg, "Dramatic Justice in *Tartuffe*", *Modern Language Notes* (May, 1975), pp. 583-590.

Montalte begs the company of this useful reinforcement for his visit, for he himself must keep to the disinterested comic role of one who "has friends in all parties".

The Dominican greets Montalte with delight ("Il fut ravi de me revoir") and that after the nonsensical conclusion and ignominious defeat of the last interview. With this good-humored, fatuous character ("le bon père", "le bon homme"), Montalte can afford to come to the point in a joshing tone. "It is enough that everyone has a *pouvoir prochain* according to which they never act; now they have a sufficient grace with which they act just as little." This is nevertheless a well-balanced, symmetrical, indisputable statement for openings. The "good Father" agrees absolutely with an admirably simple "oui". Not only that, but he spoke the full half hour allowed him in the Sorbonne to say exactly that. A rapid little interchange with Montalte that contrasts with the monk's long-windedness brings out the fact that the rule limits the length but not the brevity of speeches. Our proverb-quoting monk has missed the point of the rule completely and regrets not having spoken longer.

The Dominican has to stand alone in this scene to represent his group, and what a sorry, laughable figure he presents. Like the Jansenist, of course, he has no name but is typed by his group. The shadowy M. N. keeps his initial for a name. The Dominican continues to agree to the flat contradictions Montalte fires at him, just as the chorus bobbed their heads delightedly in the first letter: "Cela est vrai. . . . Il est vrai." Since it is difficult to get any hold on such a mushy response, Montalte sets before him a very concrete example: Could your Prior convince you that a bit of bread and a glass of water were *sufficient* for dinner by saying so?

Are you so far out of the world that you do not know the meaning of the word "sufficient"? Is it a matter of indifference whether you say that with sufficient grace one can act?

But the monk is off the track again, thrown off on a tangent by the word "indifferent"; or rather he is back on his own track, over-mastered by the idea of the power of solidarity in the group. He is scandalized; but even his sense of scandal is twisted. According to the axis of his thinking, public scandal does not enter his mind, has nothing to do with it, but only scandal within the group. "What! indifferent! It is heresy to deny it." The doctrine must be imposed on the people, though it makes no sense whatsoever. The people are made for the profession, not the profession for the people. They must be led like sheep, form to take precedence over natural intelligence, at all costs.

Montalte sees an unreal world emerging. No logical stand is possible. "I am a Jansenist if I say one thing, a *heretic*, according to you, if I say the opposite like the Jesuits, and *extravagant*, against common sense, according to the Jesuits, if I say both at once like you."

Then he sets his own axis, in the search for truth, to throw into relief the "through the looking glass" fantasy world of the Dominican: "Only the Jansenists avoid the error of the one and the folly of the other."

The Jansenist tries to get at the question of hypocrisy, with the rather politely phrased question: "Is it acting sincerely" to let people think you agree with the Jesuits because you use the term "sufficient grace", when you do not mean it as they do?

The Dominican misses the point; he has a one-track mind. "What are you complaining about? When we say openly in our schools that we do not mean the same thing?" Only the world of the Dominican schools exists for him. In the light (or darkness) of his aberration, he is so very sincere about being illogical. The Jansenist, too, tries desperately to get him out of his little world: I would have you "publish" it everywhere that you mean that sufficient grace is not sufficient, and that your meaning of the word is different from everyone else's. He resorts to parable, a more developed concrete example than Montalte's. The poor Dominican stands astonished, rendered mute (like his group in the first letter), defeated, probably, not by the unarguable logic of the illustration but by the surface authority of biblical style.

Reduced to this pitiable state, he is nevertheless prodded by Montalte's questionable sympathy and gentleness into muttering: Easy enough for you to talk; you are free to say what you please, but I belong to a religious community; I am at the mercy of the hierarchy and could be sent off in disgrace. A confessed rascal and hypocrite, pleading expediency, he can convince himself that he is honestly dishonest. He has passed the buck. He is to find no relief. The merciless Montalte still pursues his victim, asking why the group does it.

The last answer of this frustrated buffoon will provide a transition to the following letters and a frontal attack on the Jesuits. He says in effect: Do you not know our historical difficulties, although we tried to hold to Thomist doctrine and fervently opposed the appearance of the doctrine of Molina? But the Jesuits, from the beginning of the heresy of Luther and Calvin, knowing the ignorance of the people spread their doctrine and became masters of the credulous populace. If we had not appeared to agree with them, they would have condemned us like the Calvinists or treated us as the Jansenists are treated now. What could we do to save the truth without losing our reputation, except to give lip service?

He is down to the bare threads of his self-deception, unconscious of the contradiction, unaware that truth and ambition are not one and the same.

In this second attack, it is clear that between the Jesuit and the Dominican there is little choice left for morality. As the fox and the wolf differ in the *Roman de Renart* only by the degree of agile cleverness or heavy stupidity, here there is only the distinction of effective strategy as against ineffective weakness. Gallic wit attacks them indiscriminately. In inverse order, through the exposure of the weakness of one opponent, the other, the stronger, will emerge as the real enemy.

To the last ditch, the Dominican is consistent in his inconsistency. One must leave him the tatters of his cloak of jealous, misguided loyalty. He and his will suffer "martyrdom" before they will consent to "sufficient grace with the Jesuits' meaning"; even if Saint Thomas, whom they swear to follow to the death, says the opposite.

The Jansenist, whose austere shadow throws the Dominican into comic relief, is a strategist, too. He takes on the attack, though he thinks Montalte is already won over. He must get in at the kill. He will ask about sincerity when he clearly means hypocrisy. However, he wants his opponent's meaning to come out crystal clear: he should publish to the far corners of the earth that sufficient does not mean sufficient.

The Jansenist is eloquent. But do we detect repeatedly his own pride in his eloquence? Is the beloved sound of his voice apt to take hold of him and drive him? Faced with his slippery adversary, he is carried away by his exasperation and frustration into a Rabelaisian, extravagant and comprehensive multiplicity of examples of people who understand the word "sufficient" to mean one thing: all the people in the world; all women, who make up half the world; all people of the Court; all the

military; all the magistrates; all the people of the tri-
bunals; the merchants; the artisans; all the common
people. His insistence gets a bit heavy and exhausted.
Finally, probably leaning on the syllables, "all sorts
of men, except the Dominicans".

He has, of course, depth of perspective, attested in
his statement of the central question, serving as introduction to the parable. (All that is very useful to Montalte, who must not get too serious.) The parable itself
is admirably clear, concrete, and dramatic.

He is, at the same time, intransigent, pitiless, and
notably lacking in tact. "Do not flatter yourself that
you saved the truth; if it had had no other protectors,
it would have perished in such feeble hands. You have
received the enemy into the Church. Names are insep-
arable from things. The Jesuits will triumph." Thus
he forces his opponent, already down, to his last extravagant statement. This conceivably sends Montalte into
spasms of controlled laughter, for "my friend, more
serious than me" launches into his last orgy of eloquence.
All the authorities of the Church, from Christ himself
to Saint Thomas, "the angel of the school", have trans-
mitted "this victorious grace", gloriously defended
even by former Dominicans. He waxes poetic with the
vast extended ripples of his plurals and the weight of
his imperfect subjunctives. All this very long sentence
builds to climax, "to the end of time", only to fall flat
dramatically in too short an element at the end: "finds
itself abandoned for such unworthy interests." Grace
demands pure hearts disengaged from the interests of
the world. The Jansenist ends with threats that God
will snatch away the torch and leave the Dominicans
in darkness.

Obviously, he has not the restraint of the poor Dominican who at least kept to his half-hour in the Sorbonne,

for his fire was still on the upgrade ("il s'échauffa de plus en plus"). He would have continued, but all this is too much for Montalte, and he cuts him off. Of course, bombastic though it may be, Pascal got it all in by means of the Jansenist, about pure hearts and serving God for God. The comic mask is sustained, but the Montalte mask grows thin at times. The real artist, behind the players, must seem unconscious of his art but must never be so.

Aside from the four main characters, there are the four characters of the parable. The eloquence of the Jansenist's sincerity in seeking for truth (which is undeniable and which is not his comic side, just as sincerity itself is not a failing in Alceste) turns to the New Testament form which runs parallel with the sudden depth of the discussion. The narrative opens with the biblical language of the story of the good Samaritan, the traveler who fell among thieves and was left half dead. The parable, however, is transformed almost immediately into a Molière farce. The Church is likened to three physicians.

Why has so much of Molière's theater to do with doctors and patients? Why does Pascal in this critical illustration make his priests into doctors? It is, of course, simpler to understand doctors to the body than doctors to the soul, and a parable must proceed on the secular level. In lay terms, it has always seemed to me that the professions treat man in differing degrees of helplessness and frustration and that in the helplessness of man lies the essence of the human comedy. Man should be the master of his fate, and so often he is not, through exterior or surface forces. Ideas are of incalculable importance in their influence on people, but pupils seated before a professor have a built-in defense. They can just not listen or go out of the classroom and think

anything they please. The lawyer who through inept-
ness in court brings about a bad or false decision for his
client alters irreversibly to some extent the outward
course of the person's life, but the doctor—if he chooses
the wrong treatment or his knife slips, there may be no
life. The professions lend themselves to comedy in
proportionate degree. The instinct of the comedian, at
least until very recent spectacular advances in medicine,
has often gone straight and true to the doctors.

Our traveler sends for three doctors—a neat, mysterious, magic number like the three witches of *Macbeth*.
The first (no names in the little farce, but obviously a
Jansenist, an Augustinian in approach) probes, says the
wounds are fatal and only God can help. The second (the
Jesuit) flatters him, saying he has the strength to get
home. The poor patient in his dilemma holds out his
hands to the third (the Dominican) for weight of judgment on either side. The latter joins with the second
against the first and by force of numbers drives him out.
Thinking them in agreement the patient, still weak, asks
for his reasoning. "You have legs," he answers, "and
legs are enough." "But can I use them?" says the sick
man. "No, unless God helps you." To the question, "Then
you do not agree on my state?", the third doctor admits
that he does not. The patient complains of the "procédé
bizarre" and "termes ambigus", realistically tests and
confirms his own weakness, recalls the first doctor,
prays to God in humility, is accorded mercy and the
strength to get home.

The characters of the little play are sketched in their
barest lines, like the few strokes of the caricaturist.
They can carry out their capers in one act, four small
scenes of adventure, confrontation with pompous delib-
eration ending in a scuffle, frustration and the near

triumph of the charlatans, and the reversal in the happy ending.

Comedy of language.   Sense and nonsense.

Providing contrast to this terse, effective tale which is the kernel of the letter, the Jansenist's flowery oratory is not the only example of the comic effect of elevated tone. His is dignified, at least, by the exaggerated fire of an idealistic concept, made comic only by his unconscious pride in the sound of the phrases. Montalte, laughing, mocks deliberately, with the conscious irony of high words and the dignity of apostrophe to express flat, clear, bourgeois common sense, for his eyes are trained low at the moment on empty, windy words, restrained by the half-hour rule in the Sorbonne. "Oh the good rule for ignorant people! Oh the honest pretext for those who have nothing good to say!" Realistic as he is, he manages a slightly more gentlemanly tone than the Jansenist; he keeps to plurals and does not say it is the Dominican, although anyone but the Dominican would perceive the implication.

Sober irony, in the choice of words, manages flattery that is, in truth, denunciation: "In good faith, Father, this doctrine is very subtle."

One has to note the contrast of theoretical language relieved by the Father's proverb-quoting and the staccato, rapid-fire questions of Montalte, that, too, interrupted with a brief moment out for the mock-heroic. The comic pace is never allowed to flag. The lively parable cuts into the argumentation of the Jansenist, the tirade which is in itself arresting, first with the long list of people who understand what a word should mean (at the very least, imaginative) and its series of oratorical, and effective, questions. The parable, too, opens with a question to make sure his audience is alert and, at the same time, neatly putting a symbolic title on his graphic little story ("une peinture de l'Eglise").

Language on two levels has its own comic effect. The theoretical, a sufficient grace that is not sufficient, descends to the eminently practical, with bread and water that will not sufficiently nourish. The effect is heightened when we visualize the poor monk sitting before his crust and cup.

The brief transitions in this letter, that is even more completely conversation than the first one, carry their own weight for comic effect. Suggestive as before of facial expression, of the beaming countenance, the brief remark, "il fut ravi de me revoir", has the alliteration of the r's of *rire*.

Again the whole discussion turns on a word, a word divorced from its meaning, form substituted for sense. The Jansenist explains, with barely restrained impatience, "There are two things in this word of 'sufficient grace': there is the sound, which is only wind, and the thing it means, which is real and effective." One cannot give any meaning one wishes to a word or one loses contact with reality: "Did you forget, when you left the world . . . ?"

The pitying, disparaging, superiority of the terms, "the good Father", "this good man", or "odd" procedure and "ambiguous" terms, continues their effect but with restraint in their use.

The fervent words of the Dominican, "martyrdom", following "to the death", owe their comic effect not to the exaggeration but to its contrast with the lack of meaning in what he would defend, and so to that curious exaggeration which is *unwitting* frustration. He is unaware that the extravagant expressions translate to weakness and to nonsense.

It is not quite so with the sudden reversal in the direction of the Jansenist's long oratorical sentence. He does run out of wind in the last phrase, but if all his beautiful torch-bearing fizzles out into low ambition, at least he intended to end up indicating that very thing.

Montalte knows exactly what he is doing, and he is in part mimicking the Jansenist's style when he interrupts him to say to "mon Père" that he would publish "to the sound of the trumpet" that when the Jacobins say sufficient grace is given to all, they mean that all have not the grace that suffices effectively.

From that loud proclamation we drop abruptly: "Ainsi finit notre visite." End to the tale.

Epilogue: a deft play on words to turn sufficient grace into a "political sufficiency". A word of transition indicates that the act of censorship has been accomplished.[18] Events are hastening on.

The ending is sudden. The conclusion does not need to cast its little arrow into the future, as in the first letter. The depth of theme has already been added in the Jansenist's speech. All the faithful ask of the theologians, "quel est le véritable état de la nature depuis sa corruption." The true state of human nature since the fall of man is the question of the *Pensées*. The question underlines the importance of the whole discussion and makes the comedy of aberrations all the more profound. This, with the widened horizon of generality, rather than partisanship, will be the comedy of the *Pensées*.

---

18. Note by Nicole to the first *Provinciale*: "ce malicieux artifice que notre Auteur également éloquent et enjoué tourne en ridicule. . . . Il dépeint toute cette fourberie avec les couleurs les plus agréables . . . ce *pouvoir prochain* n'étoit qu'un jeu inventé pour faire hâter la Censure . . . "—*Oeuvres*, G. E. ed., IV, p. 146.

The Third *Provinciale*
Clowns: Religious and Human

A comprehensive conclusion to the two letters in the *Réponse du Provincial aux deux lettres de son ami* marks clearly the role of comedy. "Everyone sees them, everyone understands them, everyone believes them." It is the judgment of the general public, this understanding between the author and his readers of what is normal and acceptable, the measure and the screen against which the grotesque shadow of the aberrations will stand out.

The letters are "agréables aux gens du monde". The style of the *honnête homme* not only requires the light touch of comedy but would find comedy valid as a realistic approach.

The letters are "intelligible even to women". The humor of this remark is not really Pascal's but comes from the perspective of the present-day reader. Are we permitted to find here unwitting humor on the part of the author, who, in this instance, takes himself too seriously?[1] He quotes a woman who supposedly calls

1. Nicole's echo in his Note to the second *Provinciale* is not less serious: "il est indigné avec raison qu'on en use indifféremment en parlant au peuple ignorant et aux simples femmes . . . "—*Oeuvres*, G. E. ed., IV, p. 177. Sainte-Beuve reports a remark that has a touch of conscious humor: "Le cardinal Mazarin, dès les premiers jours [of the dispute in the Sorbonne], avait dit à l'évêque d'Orléans, M. d'Elbène, qu'il fallait accommoder et presser cette affaire: que les femmes ne

the letters "une délicate et innocente censure". And the censure involved is really not always so delicate and hardly innocent. Pascal does not hesitate to use women in this "Réponse du Provincial" to help his mask of comedy not to slip and to help assure that his armor of the teasing form, as well as his anonymity, shall be as secure as possible from direct attack.[2]

The remedy of comedy, laughter, destroys the threat to social solidarity. "These words of *pouvoir prochain* and *grâce suffisante* . . . will no longer make us afraid." Irony realistically disposes of the "solidity" of these empty words.

The opponents, the masters who manipulate the people, are revealed in their sham and emptiness ("Nous avons trop appris des Jésuites, des Jacobins et de M. Le Moine") and stripped of their ominous grimace, as they are laughed at.

This *Réponse du Provincial* (with its imaginary date),

---

faisaient qu'en parler, quoiqu'elles n'y entendissent rien, non plus que lui"—*Pascal et Port-Royal*, in Pascal, *Les Provinciales* (Paris: Nouvel Office d'Edition, 1964), p. 12.

2. It is to be noted that this did not escape the contemporaries. An exaggerated, acrid, and malicious reaction comes from Marandé, the King's Counselor in *Considérations sur un Libelle du Port-Royal* . . . , dated March 20, 1656: "[M. Arnauld] . . . s'avise dans cette troisième Lettre de monter sur le Theatre, et de faire le Comique sous la representation d'un Hermaphrodite, qui pour sujet de son entrée s'est proposé d'annoncer les éloges et les louanges incomparables que mérite Mr Arnauld dans ses deux premières gazettes. . . . Il paroist ensuite . . . sous un visage féminin, coquet, poudré, musqué, et si mignard, que l'Assemblée est toute surprise de ce soudain changement. Et comme les louanges des Dames ont quelque chose de plus charmant et de plus delicat que celles des hommes, cette mignonne joignant le son de sa voix à celuy des paroles, produit une si douce harmonie dans le recit des eloges miraculeux, qu'elle donne à l'Auteur de ces belles gazettes, que peut s'en faut que toute l'assistance n'en demeure pâmée . . . " (Pascal, *Oeuvres*, G. E. ed., V, p. 8).

actually published with the third letter, provides transition to a wider attack.

The arrangement of the third letter is again very different from the preceding one, with a new flavor of generalization and vaster horizons half emerging —thence the possibility of new uses for comedy.

Characters. Larger than life.

The setting is in a way very dissimilar, with an epic suggestion of massed characters behind any one shadowy figure, like a frieze. The effect is of a widening audience as well as of widening spiritual implication.

The characters are few and strangely undelimited. There is M. Arnauld, who does not appear, but who speaks, through the quotes of Montalte; Arnauld represents all the victims, the Jansenists. The Jesuits, the Molinists, speak, too, but secondhand, through the mouth of Montalte, and are referred to in the third person both by him and by the neutral, as the principal subjects in his narration. And who is this neutral, with his crowd behind him, "un de ceux qui furent neutres", neutral in the first question but not in the second? The indifferent ones were the smallest number in the first letter. The neutral here takes on more importance: he has the one main scene with Montalte and does most of the talking in it. Does he represent the "indifférents", that most difficult segment of the audience to whom the *Apologie* would be directed? (Montalte also mentions the atheists: "les idolâtres et les athées".) Montalte, himself, present throughout, does all the narrating of one-half of the main part of the letter, as well as the introduction and the conclusion. Has he come to represent more clearly, by his common sense, the great mass of the people? Note the equilibrium in the frieze, the victims and the persecutors set against each other, but, then, superimposed, Montalte and the "indifférent".

The epic view should not come to us as a surprise. There is a childlike wonderment in the epic vein as in the comic view of the scheme of things.

Montalte does identify himself with all of Christendom, "Toute la chrétienté", which is waiting, wide-eyed, for the Sorbonne to show the "imperceptible point" of difference between the pronouncements of Arnauld and the Fathers of the Church. The epic suggestion does no harm to the comic drop from the sublime to the ridiculous but only deepens it. It is not the mock-heroic approach, applied in the first and second letters to more concrete adversaries in the immediate conflict. Here everyone ("tout le monde") waited with bated breath to learn what diversity existed, but everyone was frustrated in "our" expectation ("notre attente"). All the public is ringed around for instruction, as in an amphitheater. All this audience shares, for the moment, Montalte's assumed role of naïveté. With him they also ask probing questions and suffer his frustration. They do not share his role of master of ceremonies, which he sustains as before, prodding the neutral one with ironic half-agreement: "J'admire leur prudence et leur politique . . . rien de plus judicieux ni de plus sûr." He manages his puppets with a deft hand; needing fewer questions than before, but questions immediately to the point.

The neutral is disabused and indulges in the sophisticated raillery of an Ecclesiastes ("Vanity of vanities") and derisive laughter at naïve and idealistic belief in good faith: "How simple you are to believe a difference exists." ("Que vous êtes simple de croire. . . . ") He enjoys the spectacle of it: "comme s'il eût pris plaisir. . . . "He is versed in the ways of the Jesuits and their policy of expediency; indeed, he takes it for granted and takes a bitter pleasure in explaining the details of strategy. Montalte concludes that this neutral would not have been indifferent, however, to the question[3] of why the Jesuits proceed on no evidence at all. For this indifferent man is intelligent; he will not have his power of reasoning insulted. He comes up with a knowledgeable if disillusioned basis for their action. The Jesuits are opportunists, their censure is useful to them, and it will work for a time. Why should it not? As long as they shout it in the streets, people will believe. How many will read the account? How few of those will understand it? How few will notice that it does not answer to the point? Who do you think cares (" . . . qui prenne les choses à coeur") or undertakes to examine closely? Even silence (it is cleverest to say little so that there is nothing to take hold of) is a mystery for the simple ones. In the term "les simples" lies his scornful attack, not on the cleverness of the Molinists who manipulate the people in this comedy and move them about like pawns on a chessboard of political power, but on the blindness and apathy of the public that allows itself to be duped, to be moved about like so many objects.

Yet the laugh is turned on this scornful man, too, by the reader, for Pascal has seen to it that the reader shall understand. The depth of the indifferent man's skepticism betrays his disappointment, and the word liberty is on his lips, even if the expression is a negative one. The half-hour rule, the means to insure lack of liberty, will work against the Jesuits in the end. People will know that seventy doctors who have nothing to gain by defending M. Arnauld will count more than a hundred who have

3. The Grands Ecrivains edition assumes "la première question [de fait]" and "la seconde [de droit]" (IV, p. 191), but such an inference in the text of this letter does not seem clear.

nothing to lose by condemning him. The neutral man laughs at the boomerang: the force of numbers will be reversed; reason will triumph in the end; the deceiver will be deceived.

M. Arnauld comes out the innocent, the lamb led to slaughter, in this parody of a morality play, "une procession où la grâce suffisante mène l'efficace en triomphe", a parody even of a miracle play, "une comédie où les diables emportent Jansénius". The word comedy is out, spoken in his apparent detachment by the "indifférent". The comic effect is not lessened by the fact that the means used against the Jansenists, the "catéchisme", the "procession", the "comédie", the "almanach", are references to actual fact.[4] If the catechism was intended seriously, with its required answer from the pupils that the Jansenists were the greatest heretics (one can hear the children's muffled giggles), the "procession" was a bit of foolery in its own right "faite dans les rues de Mâcon en 1651, le lundi gras, par les écoliers des Jesuites . . . ". In answer to the Jesuit schoolboy's jest, the pupils at Port-Royal drowned dolls representing Escobar in the canal of their abbey. The "comedy", Nicole noted, was a tragedy presented at the Collège de Clermont. The Almanach of 1653 included *la Déroute et la Confusion des Jansénistes*. The facts were known to the readers and appreciated, giving them a fine sense of superior awareness. These are the kinds of political jokes, allusions to current events, used by comedians in vaudeville or in nightclubs.

The word "frustrated" comes out, too, to maintain the comic situation of M. Arnauld and the Jansenists massed behind him. The act of censuring the propositions "a bien frustré notre attente". The people, with Montalte, ally themselves with M. Arnauld at this moment in their

4. See *Oeuvres*, G. E. ed., IV, p. 219.

comic disappointment at this abrupt dashing of their
hopes. They are disgruntled ("la plupart des gens . . .
sont entrés en mauvaise humeur"). Gesture is suggested,
as it is in the exclamation, "Eh quoi!"; one can see their
faces. They hold a grudge, finding themselves in a
topsy-turvy world and put upon: they draw from the
conduct of the censors "admirable" consequences to
prove the innocence of M. Arnauld. M. Arnauld is so
innocent that he does not even defend himself but leaves
that to Montalte. He draws the sympathy of the under-
dog, with its implications of condescending and amused
pity: "tant de docteurs si acharnés sur un seul".

The Jesuits, of course, are the "diables". They are
behind the scenes, too, in their play within the play. No
detail of their actions is missed in the cynical account
of the neutral or in the report of Montalte. The triple
list of the Jesuits' denunciations is evidence of how
angry they become, and their anger creates comic
vulnerability ("Voilà de quelle sorte ils s'emportent").
Montalte's ironic comment that they are "trop péné-
trants" does not even imply hairsplitting but rather
that they are obtuse, drawing about them the cloak
of their false scholarly dignity (the ironic "Voulons-
nous être plus savants que messieurs nos maîtres?")
against impertinence that will translate the censure
itself to heresy ("Il ne faudrait rien pour rendre cette
censure hérétique").

The neutral states more directly, with his superior
laugh, that these clowns make no pretense of coherence
in their practice. They just beat their opponent over
the head. They want to attack Arnauld; he says nothing
wrong; then they just condemn without saying about
what or why. What need of a pretext? You think they
would not have been delighted to publish a reason if
there were one? It is attack or be overcome: they are

pressed furiously by the Jansenists, and volumes over-
whelm them when they say the least word out of line with
tradition. One can see the Jesuits chasing the Jansenist
around the ring ("Ils ont jugé . . . plus facile de censurer
que de repartir"): "It is easier to find monks than reasons."[5] Any means at hand, any ritual, or comedy, or
censorship will suffice to divert the audience and dull
their curiosity as to who should really be coming out
on top.

Montalte delivers the final terse comment: I admire
their prudence and their politics; only the person of M.
Arnauld is heretical, not what he says. Political strategy
is the point, along with pure prejudice and defamation
of character. These are the tactics of the "devils".

Structure. The Foolish foiled.

In the structure of this letter, as in the characters,
an antithetical element emerges with almost static
equilibrium. The brief introduction and the equally
brief conclusion, by Montalte, each have one long and
one short paragraph, remarkably adjusted in length.
The long flashback, by Montalte, his exposition, which
is in itself dramatic (as in the first letter), and the main
scene with the neutral are solidly developed and of
equal length. Malherbe could not ask for more "archi-
tectural proportions". Order laughs behind the scenes
in this little universe that presents a picture of disorder.
The puppet actors dance on the rigged stage. They are
alive, they talk: the whole is in vivid conversation.

In situations, within the overall structure, frustration
is the order of the day. The introduction spells out what

5. Which the Prince de Guemené " . . . fait passer comme en prov-
erbe . . . quand on luy donne une mauvaise raison, il dit aussitôt *voilà
un moine*, et quand on luy donne une bonne raison, voilà une raison,
mais l'autre est un moine"—*Ouevres*, G. E. ed., IV, p. 217.

is to come: Montalte was all prepared to hear of terrible heresies and they all explode to nothing ("que tant d'éclatantes préparations se soient anéanties") just when they should have burst into a brilliant spectacle. Such monumental effort to no purpose; such running around to get nowhere. The short paragraph has a double laugh: Montalte mocking both himself and the awkward ineffectiveness of the Jesuits.

In the flashback, after the blown-up and empty accusations against the Jansenists, one drops abruptly to the realistic statement of the problem, as in the first letter. Some thought of looking at their books ("on a pris le dessein d'examiner leurs livres pour en faire le jugement"). We are in the courtroom: action! drama! They chose the second letter of M. Arnauld. The action rises in merriment. Even this concrete point of departure cannot hold the Jesuits to reality. They are off again, into superlatives of prejudice and defamation. They stack the examining board with his most declared enemies. They try to ferret out errors. And M. Arnauld's letter is so in line with the Fathers of the Church that *no one* can see any difference. There is no point; then they have to imagine one. At this the wide-eyed public and Montalte, who have let out their breath since their expectation was all for nothing, do not now know where to put a foot. They want to find the evil in order to detest it. But all they can see is these buffoons of censors tripping themselves up and proving M. Arnauld's innocence ("Ils tirent des conséquences admirables pour l'innocence de M. Arnauld"). The spectators are nonplussed at the unwitting frustration of the Molinists. At the same time, to look any further into the specious pretext of an existing difference might be to stumble on the truth and come out venerating what, in docile good faith, they are trying to hate. Everybody is frustrated.

Montalte, in neat transition, goes off in bewilderment to find one of the neutrals.

The latter, cynical idealist that he is, vents his spleen in sneering laughter, parades his superior detachment and knowledge of a man of the world, and then cannot keep the word liberty off his vulnerable and wistful lips. The people whom he despises for their simplicity will shortly come out on top, for there are "those who are not dupes". Yet our sophisticate must save face and go on admiring "the machines of Molinism"[6] and tell Montalte to do so, in this upside-down, rigged world.

At this point, he exits ("Sur cela il me quitta"). End of scene.

Montalte draws the conclusion. Definitions do not count. Heresy is not a belief. It is a person. Therefore, the best way to destroy Molinism would be for Arnauld to defend it. This bewildering, frustrating jumble has nothing to do with theology but only with these fools of theologians. He goes off laughing and shaking his head. And signs a string of initials that are admittedly confusing but do have meaning. With his departing wink, the Montalte mask slips a little.

Comedy of language. The cosmic twist.

Within this balanced, statuesque, ironic frieze the comedy of words, syntax, tone, comes into its own. It is as though, in this virtuosity of comic language, Pascal willingly allows the fire of words to take hold of him.

Antitheses reign from the first moment. Montalte says: M. Arnauld must make himself known to defend his innocence, and I must keep my anonymity so as not to lose my reputation. Rational order is reversed, and he

---

6. See the *Défense* attributed to Nicole: "Qu'on remuast toutes sortes de machines"—*Oeuvres*, G. E. ed., IV, p. 118. The comedy is brought out by Pascal, in the ambivalent attitude of the neutral.

laughs at conditions that are the opposite of the appro-
bation in the answering letter from his friend. It is a
jumbled heap of antitheses, spelling disorder. You take
care of my famous fans, he exhorts him, and I will inform
you of the censure of my detractors (which presents
even more disorder).

Montalte was "extremely surprised". He expected the
most "horrible heresies", with breathless alliteration
that amounts to onomatopaeia in this first and only
superlative of the introduction. In the same sentence
these brilliant preparations (expressed in a sheaf of
explosive consonants, "que tant d'éclatantes préparations") kill themselves off with the abrupt and dynamic
diminution of the verb ("se soient anéanties"). The verb
itself has nothingness in it. This constant buildup
through the letter ("Ils tirent de leur conduite des conséquences admirables") and the abrupt letdown, the
descent to reality, often within the same sentence ("pour
l'innocence de M. Arnauld") are the syntax of frustration,
of the monumental effort for nothing.

This dignified rhythm of fizzling out expresses also
the laughable frustration of astonishment. Comic astonishment has an active value, only half felt here, in the
triumphant assertion of "l'innocence de M. Arnauld".
It is a constant technique as well as a constant, sincere
reaction of Pascal's, which remains and reverses itself
in the dynamic paradoxes of the *Pensées*. Those, we shall
note, will spiral skyward, with metaphors mingling to
produce the rising veil of smoke that destroys contradiction on one level to clear into new syntheses on another plane, producing new paradox. Pascal's abrupt
burst of laughter breaks out repeatedly at the strange-
ness of reality (we note his frequent use of the words
"bizarre" and "étrange": "les étranges impressions qu'on
nous donne des Jansénistes"). One feels in him a spon-

taneous, intellectual joy in the problem, as well as recurrent disillusionment in the realization of the human being's half-sight ("Now I see as in a glass darkly").

There are two elements here. One is incongruity, a valid wellspring of laughter. Things just do not go together on the surface.

There is also the strange delight of pure surprise, the spontaneous child's laugh that captivates Baudelaire.[7] At each new perspective Pascal sees on the surface, with a childlike wonder and freshness. He has a very profound and conscious use for the specious naïveté of Montalte. M. Béguin has said in another context: "L'une des forces de Pascal . . . c'est la nature si juvénile de son génie. On oublie trop qu'il est mort très tôt. . . . "[8] To the end of his short life Pascal keeps and uses an initial childlike wonder. It would be a mistake to forget the basic element of joy in laughter.[9]

For the child looks first without judgment, thence his true comic detachment. Like Pascal he is an obvious realist. He has in his mind no "emperor's clothes" to cloak the nudity of things as they are on the surface. Is not this also the eternal wonder of the scientific approach that continued to fascinate Pascal and that has enthralled humankind through the last four centuries? There are two stages in the quest for comprehension: first, the delighted contemplation of the multiplicity of forms; then the search, an intellectual delight in itself ("la recherche" of Pascal's *Pensées*). It is a joyous search, however much it is accompanied with groaning ("ceux qui cherchent en gémissant"), for the essential unity of

7. "Le rire des enfants . . . est la joie de recevoir, la joie de respirer, la joie de s'ouvrir, la joie de contempler, de vivre, de grandir"—*De l'essence du rire*, p. 984.

8. Albert Béguin, *Pascal par lui-même* (Paris: Seuil, 1958), p. 5.

9. Is not this allied in spirit with the profound childlike humility noted by his confessor in the last stage of his life?

things, "la vérité", order, rationality, unity in truth.

This is the valid, profound, comic approach of both the *Provinciales* and the *Pensées*. If the *Provinciales* are an attack on corruption in the very center of the institution of the Church, in its leaders and teachers, the Jesuits, the *Pensées* are an attack on the same tendencies in all human beings, the vanity of "le moi haïssable". There is but a step from one to the other. It is the inevitable step taken by the spectator of a Molière play who laughs wholeheartedly at the antics of the actors and, only in walking up the aisle to leave the theater, says to himself, "Whom was I laughing at? Was it I? What play am I playing in?"

Just so the stages of comic approach and technique have their own durable, artistic beauty. Baudelaire says of truly great caricature: "les autres . . . contiennent un élément mystérieux, durable, éternel, qui les recommande à l'attention des artistes. Chose curieuse et vraiment digne d'attention que l'introduction de cet élément insaisissable du beau jusque dans les oeuvres destinées à représenter à l'homme sa propre laideur morale et physique!" This paradox of beauty in the representation of ugliness carries its own childlike wonder and astonishment at incongruity for the poet, whose manner of thinking falls so directly into the line of Pascal's: "Et chose non moins mystérieuse, ce spectacle lamentable excite en lui une hilarité immortelle et incorrigible."[10]

Comedy must divert, and Pascal, the *honnête homme*, intends to make understanding easy and pleasant for the reader ("Pour l'entendre avec plaisir").

Though some of the techniques of comic language are the same as previous ones, nevertheless, as Montalte

10. "Voilà donc le véritable sujet de cet article"—*De l'essence du rire*, p. 976.

goes into his dramatic flashback, the picture is different. The rhythm of buildup and letdown that holds
through the letter converges gradually upon the Jesuits
as a focal point. We do not have here a general parade of
pomp and circumstance as in the first letter, but the
buildup will be used to paint the barrage of enemy fire
that turns out to be only fireworks.

The irony of the familiar conversational tone that
leans hard upon empty expressions for emphasis serves
to make the exaggeration of the opponents' attack seem
all the more ineffective: "*tant* d'éclatantes préparations
. . . depuis *si* longtemps . . . depuis *si* longtemps . . .
combien ce torrent . . . *tant* de violence . . . *tant*
d'accusations si atroces . . . ".[11] The expression "ces
bons Molinistes" is used once; it has little pity in it, for
already they are not good at all. Irony becomes very
pointed: whether they were too scornful to come down
from their lofty heights to explain or from some other
"secret" reason. "Secret" here can mean nonexistent, or
sheer prejudice, or, more malevolently, deliberate intent.
The mechanical time-limit for speeches, used against
verbosity in the first letter, becomes here a restriction
on liberty of speech, with the irony of inflated language
for a petty tactic: "cette rare et nouvelle invention de la
demi-heure et du sable". Directed against those who
would reason, attack the Jesuits' reasoning, and reduce
them to not being able to retort, the hourglass represents
"ce manquement de liberté", a cutting off of debate, a
strangling of opposition, a tyranny of power.

The crescendo of attack from the Jesuits begins with
a list of horrors: "les cabales, les factions, les erreurs,
les schismes, les attentats", five giant shots as in a
Rabelaisian war, somewhat equal to each other in an
abstract way, and activated by the force of verbs: the

11. The italics are mine.

Jansenists are "decried and blackened, orally and in
books." For a moment one rests on a balanced plane
("non seulement hérétiques et schismatiques, mais
apostats et infidèles") only to rise higher: "to deny the
mystery of transubstantiation and to renounce Jesus
Christ and the Scriptures". One descends abruptly to
the examination of texts. Then a jack-in-the-box rising
again to the attack: M. Arnauld's proposition is met with
a piling up of epithets, five: "téméraire, impie, blas-
phématoire, frappé d'anathème, et hérétique".[12] They
are down: they have proved only M. Arnauld's innocence.
But the two lists of horrors merge to pepper the Jansenists with "all the most terrible terms" (appropriate
alliteration of explosives), now doubled in number: "de
poison, de peste, d'horreur, de témérité, d'impiété, de
blasphème, d'abomination, d'exécration, d'anathème,
d'hérésie", terms fit for the annihilation of an antichrist.
How Pascal has used and increased in effect the "comme
une peste . . . cette pernicieuse et pestilente doctrine"
of the *Censure*.[13] One can enjoy the all-out sound of
the language and the irony of each epithet that in reality
disparages not the Jansenists, but the Jesuits in their
unmitigated prejudice. Poison and plague are a boomerang, and the attack goes round and round.

The "machines du molinisme" produce an upside-down
world where what is catholic in the Fathers of the Church
becomes heretic in M. Arnauld, and the ancient doctrine
of St. Augustine is "an unbearable novelty". M. Le Moine,
"the most ardent of the examiners", is reported as admiring this state of affairs in all seriousness.

The waves of attack that rise higher and higher,

12. Underlined by Pascal, because it is quoted from the *Censure
de la Sacrée Faculté de Theologie de Paris, contre un Livre intitulé,
Seconde Lettre* (1656)—*Oeuvres*, G. E. ed., IV, p. 184.

13. *Oeuvres*, G. E. ed., IV, p. 186.

signalling "l'essence des plus noires hérésies", break on the sand of an "imperceptible" heresy. Since no one could find any divergence between Arnauld's text and the Fathers of the Church, one had to "imagine" a terrible difference ("On s'imaginait . . . une terrible"). Terms here begin to group themselves as though the language is taking hold of Pascal as a springboard for creation. The second "liasse" of the *Pensées*, entitled *Vanité*, carries the long picturesque passage on *Imagination (Pensées*, 44).[14] The comedy of self-deception, the deepest meaning of the *dupeur dupé*, is expressed here in the power of the imagination.

In the letter, all Christendom waits for the Sorbonne to show "ce point imperceptible au commun des hommes". "Ce point imperceptible" is repeated. "La vérité est si délicate", and "La distance en est si insensible, que j'ai eu peur", and "cette erreur est si déliée que sans même s'en éloigner, on se trouve dans la vérité".

It is still a W. C. Fields' frustration, holding through since the first letter,[15] and it is so in the *Pensées*. It is the blunt rubber dagger, the ineffective instrument, too "soft" ("mousses") to reach the objective: "La justice et la vérité sont deux pointes si subtiles que nos instruments sont trop mousses pour y toucher exactement. S'ils y arrivent ils en écachent la pointe et appuient tout autour plus sur le faux que sur le vrai" (*Pensées*, 44. "Imagination"). Our instruments "flatten, deform, shatter" ("écachent") the "points" and deflect to all the wrong places. In the *Provinciale* one stumbles on truth; in the *pensée*, one stumbles on error, all in the same human bumbling progress.

One recalls the question in the second letter: "Tous

14. All references to the *Pensées* are to the Lafuma edition of the *Oeuvres complètes*, l'Intégrale (Paris: Seuil, 1963).
15. See p. 19.

les fidèles demandent aux théologiens quel est le véritable état de la nature depuis sa corruption." In this third
letter Pascal is playing with words, words which group
themselves in his mind and take on a very different
perspective in the *Pensées*. The perspective of infinity
is not here, but it is in the *Pensées*. Imperceptible in the
letter means nonexistent, the point of attack, "un spécieux
prétexte". In "Disproportion de l'homme" (*Pensées*, 199)
what is this "point imperceptible"? "La terre lui paraisse
comme un *point* [the italics are mine] au prix du vaste
tour que cet astre décrit . . . il *s'étonne* de ce que ce
vaste tour . . . n'est qu'une pointe très *délicate*. . . .
Tout le monde visible n'est qu'un trait *imperceptible*. . . .
Qu'est-ce qu'un homme dans l'infini?" The point is so
small that it disappears, it exists only relatively, and in
relativity it is diminished to nothingness.

The comedy of blown-up self importance in the doctors
of theology parallels the comedy of humankind, through
the tricks of imagination, of self-deception, or in traditional terms, original sin: "Le péché originel . . . sans
cela, que dira-t-on qu'est l'homme? Tout son état dépend
de ce point imperceptible" (*Pensées*, 695). The willful
blindness of the teachers of the Church and the willful
blindness of the human being are a constant marvel to
Pascal ("il s'étonne"). The words that cloak the idea
carry their comic value into different domains. Are
they really so different? Christendom looks to the
Sorbonne for enlightenment and does not find it. One
must look within oneself for the kingdom of God, but
there, too, one is easily deceived.

The Fourth *Provinciale*
Through the Looking Glass

Structure.   The duel: the Jesuit against all challengers.

The construction of the fourth letter raises it to a new level of comedy. The introduction and conclusion are very condensed, even shorter than in the third letter. The one paragraph of introduction sets the characters, who are now narrowed down to three, gives the setting as one interview with the Jesuit, allowing for distinct unity of time, place, and action, and presents the problem, *la grâce actuelle*, the central question of immediate grace involving action. The first sentence places the Jesuit in the spotlight as the comic character ("Il n'est rien tel que les Jésuites"). Montalte does not seek out one of the most knowledgeable, or one of the most profound, but a clever one ("un des plus habiles"), as he had talked with a very clever neutral ("un fort habile"); this is the dominating, distorting characteristic, as one might fix a title, *le Misanthrope* or *le Tartuffe*.

The conclusion, after the Jesuit's hurried exit, is equally brief, sets a repetitive tone of astonishment, and announces the subject of the next letter. Montalte is astonished that the doctrine has turned morality upside-down, and the Jansenist is astonished at his astonishment. We are going around in circles but are due to come out with an insistence on morality, on practice. The Jansenist indicates many more excesses in morality than in doctrine.

61

It is intriguing to note the evidence for the Chevalier
de Méré's suggestion (this "bel esprit de profession")
that a discussion of grace would not get to everyone
("Vous n'y êtes pas encore, mon cher"), that one needed
a bit more joy and diversion: "il faut quelque chose de
plus rejouissant, et, si vous voulez attirer l'attention
des honnestes gens, il faut les divertir. . . . "[1] En-
chanted with the first *Provinciales*, he wants more fun:
"Que n'attaquez-vous ces Casuistes. . . . "[2] More
interesting is the answer reported from Pascal, "who
rather did what he wanted with his wit": [Il] "l'entendit
à demy-mot 'Laissez-moy faire, dit-il, vous aurez con-
tentement. . . . ' "

It does seem from the evidence of the fourth letter that
Pascal was getting to this point in any case, that his
direction was inevitable as he gradually converged,
in the first letters, upon his target, and then, through
the practical consequences of doctrine, proceeded to
the political source in the King's confessor. The Jansenist insists that this Jesuit runs to the type of the "casuistes", of the "nouveaux scolastiques". Montalte's
admonition to the Jesuit is clear: "prenez garde, mon
Père, aux dangereuses suites de votre maxime." This
is the letter, too, where Pascal mentions "le P. Annat",
as the Jesuit offers the ultimate authority ("voulez-vous
une authorité plus authentique?"), and Montalte utters
his ironic "selon le P. Annat". Nicole's note to the first
Provinciale indicated the storm center: "la faveur du P.
Annat qui est la source de cette tempête".[3] For the
moment Pascal centers on the Jesuits: "Les autres ne

---

1. From the *Entretiens de Cléandre et d'Eudoxe* of Père Daniel—
Pascal, *Oeuvres*, G. E. ed., IV, p. 229.

2. Preface of l'abbé Massillon to a *Lettre du R. P. d'Aubenton, jesuite* of Sept. 9, 1713—*Oeuvres*, G. E. ed., IV, p. 230.

3. *Oeuvres*, G. E. ed., IV, p. 147.

font que les copier. Les choses valent toujours mieux dans leur source." The gradual direction is as inevitable as Voltaire's, whose attack on government meant inexorably attack on the Church.

The structure of each letter shows successive convergence. The fourth letter is high comedy that enters almost immediately into action, through constant conversation. The action is psychological, that is, intellectual with moral implications. It is a duel now, an adventure, with the joy of the intellectual contest, and carried on according to the rules, but a life and death struggle just the same, since it is a question of faith. The comedy grows more profound.

Characters. The clown through the eyes of the realist.

In the duel, Montalte and the Jansenist, "mon second", who was with him in the skirmish with the Jacobins, prod (each in his own manner) and pursue the Jesuit, who has the center of the stage.

Montalte is ironically polite ("vous m'obligeriez infiniment"), asking for a definition not in terms of the defined; and he is pained: the Jesuit could have done that in the beginning. He is continually amazed (he cannot believe his ears, "Qui pourra croire . . . ") and frank with his friend: "Are there any others who talk like him?" He is contemptuous of the casuists, the new scholastics, if they are contrary to tradition. He is incredulous at the quotations: "Voilà qui commence bien . . . voilà une rédemption toute nouvelle." He hazards broader and broader irony, in his exclamations, thus exposing the simplicity of his opponent: "O que cela me plaît! que j'en vois de belles conséquences!" He is mischievous and a bit malicious: "une fausse joie?" He teases, as much as to say, "Here we go again, riding off in no direction": "J'appréhende . . . le *distinguo.*" He might get away with that if he did not take over the Jansenist's pointed attack of the second letter: "Parlez-vous sincèrement?" (You do not mean it!) He has ruffled the good Father's feathers, and he backtracks in mock-seriousness, soothingly, to keep this marionette dancing: I am wary because I want so much to understand ("Je crains à force de désirer"). He is in constant collusion with the Jansenist's sly asides ("Mais toutes modernes, me dit doucement mon Janséniste"). It would take a change of facial expression from a quirk of the lips to wide-open eyes to reflect his ironical delight: Oh, I must bring my friends; if one cannot sin without thinking of God, they have no sins because they never think of God. He exerts himself to pin the man down: It is a funny thing that a Jansenist is a heretic for denying that a deliberate sinner is remorseful ("C'est une plaisante chose d'être hérétique pour cela!"). Are you not afraid, he says in effect, that the sinners, who know from their own experience, will not believe you in anything? He can be high-handed and put tact aside: "I must in conscience disabuse you."

He is realistic. He wants to go back to common sense: This is a question of fact; we know it ("Nous le voyons, nous le savons, nous le sentons"). He advances with agility and presses his advantage when the Jesuit shifts ground: You gave up the general principle ("Vous reculez . . . vous reculez . . . vous abandonnez le principe général"). He stands off and laughs when the Jansenist and the Jesuit fall into temporary agreement ("Voilà la première fois . . . que je vous ai vus d'accord") and spurs his friend on when the Jansenist presses for further definition. He spars with blunt examples: What about swearing and debauchery? They are not sins, then, if the sinner has not been reflecting on good and evil.

His "second" in the duel, "mon Janséniste" (the possessive here means "on my side") is very useful to Montalte. He goes along with him, bolsters his arguments ("soutenant mon discours"), and he has made all preparations for the encounter: "he had studied the whole question that very morning, so ready was he on everything." In the beginning as at the end he is surprised that Montalte did not know all this: "Cela vous est-il si nouveau?" It is a disabused attack, like the neutral's in the third letter, on the existing, already widespread corruption. He exchanges looks with Montalte ("je me tournai vers mon Janséniste, et je connus bien à sa façon qu'il n'en croyait rien"). There are plenty of others ("un beau nombre"), he says, like this one, casuists and "new" scholastics. He agrees that they have no ground to stand on in tradition. The first text, of which the Jesuit is so proud, he notes was "condemned in Rome" and by the bishops of France. Is this a dry suggestion that the condemnation, rather than the book's intrinsic value, might account for enough popularity for a "fifth edition"? To the Jesuit's "other authorities" he counters, "But all modern." When Montalte has offered his rational, common sense arguments, the Jansenist abandons his asides and takes over with his specialty of doctors and cures; one remembers his parable of the second letter. He has his own trenchant wit ("You would do well, Father, not to explain so clearly as you have to us what you mean by *grâce actuelle*") and goes on to show the glaring inconsistency. He is still eloquent and likes the sound of a multiplicity of examples, but his list is very telling. When Montalte breaks in on what seems to him the blatant stupidity of the Jesuit and protests the evidence of his common sense, the Jansenist has the courage and the wit to take on the opponent on his own ground ("se tenant dans les termes que le Père avait proscrits").

He is indeed well prepared with examples from Scripture and cuts the ground from under his opponent not
only in respect to the irreligious but for the righteous,
too. He plays according to the rules, but he presses the
Jesuit hard. He is a stickler for exact construction to be
put on texts and as knowledgeable about Aristotle as
about his Bible; he will not have the philosopher quoted
in part and out of context.

Against these two formidable and gay musketeers the
Jesuit is in real difficulty, but unfailingly optimistic; he
has, after all, only to call on the power behind him.
Though from the beginning one cannot be convinced
that he really wants to reveal anything, he expresses
great willingness: "Très volontiers . . . je le veux bien"
and a disarming "J'aime les gens curieux", which he
seems to believe himself. *La grâce actuelle* is the inspiration to accomplish God's will, and all men have it at each
temptation or their actions could not be called sins. The
Jansenists say that sins committed without it are still
sins, "but they are dreamers". While the listeners try
to brush the cobwebs out of that explanation so mag-
nanimously offered, the Jansenist could well give the
classic response: "There *is* a dreamer around here and
it is not I." The echo does come later; the Jesuit, driven
unquestionably into a corner, "après avoir un peu rêvé",
turns to Aristotle for support, only to have it proved
that, in his dream world, he does not know his Aristotle
very well. Asked for a definition not in the terms of the
word defined, he offers happily, in effect, that a sin is
not a sin unless one knew that it was wrong and was
inspired to avoid it, which leaves Montalte not knowing
what to do with all the sins that come upon us unaware.
Pressed for proof the Father is more than willing: "Laissez-moi faire." (One thinks of Pascal's supposed response
to the Chevalier de Méré, above.) He scurries off to come

back laden down with books. His first text is from *le Père* Bauny's, which has to be a good book because it is in its fifth edition. Montalte reads aloud and is not impressed, but Pascal puts the implied criticism into the good Father's own foolish mouth: one critic, M. Hallier, said, "before he was one of our friends", that that would take away all the sins in the world. Obviously, the group reformed the critic and brainwashed him of all his power of rational thinking.

With delight, the Jesuit advances a stronger authority in Father Annat—whose lines are all gold ("toutes d'or") and all inclusive—to the effect that neither omission of good actions nor commission of guilty ones is sinful if one was not thinking of God. The Jesuit lacks all sense of humor when he perceives some disbelief ("Il n'en faut pas railler"); he finds all that he is reading very straight-forward and creditable. In addition, the evidence of M. Le Moine gives such a detailed program of states of the soul to precede an act that can be called a sin that the world could indeed have few sinners. This is to be taken as admirably set forth, though not original ("Il l'a appris de nous"), says the Father condescendingly but amiably. Montalte concludes logically that half-sinners who have some idea of right will be damned and hardened sinners saved. The Jesuit is not so dense nor so far gone that he does not see the trap he has set up for himself, but, on the spur of the moment, he skips aside adroitly ("adroite-ment"): we say that all men want to do the right thing, and only the Jansenists say the opposite. When the Jan-senist states some powerful examples in philosophers, Epicureans, idolaters, and atheists, the Jesuit stoutly maintains that all these are properly inspired to pray to the true God. Besides, he says, you cannot by Scripture prove that this is not so. This is his childish response instead of either proof or accepting the logical sequence of ideas, and one can imagine with what a childish, triumphant smile he is saying, in effect, "Now I have caught you!"

Faced with the Jansenist's telling examples from Scripture, the Jesuit, knowing he opened the door for exactly that, gives ground, tosses the irreligious to the winds ("laissant pécher les impies sans inspiration"), and tries to hold fast to the righteous. He is not allowed to get the words out of his mouth; he cannot finish his sentence for interruption. Both his adversaries pounce on him, Montalte with devilish delight and the Jansenist with dignified composure, saying that even the saints admit that they do not know their own sins. Deprived of support in the sinners and the righteous, undaunted, the Father turns happily to Aristotle ("you would have to burn up the books of this prince of philosophers or be of our opinion"), only to find that Aristotle cannot support him either (though for some reason he expected to win Montalte over: "me serrant les doigts"), since the Jansenist takes the philosopher over to his side. This betrayal hits hardest. Trying valiantly to think of something, he is rescued, summoned by two aristocratic ladies, and goes off in understandable haste. He will talk to his cohorts ("à nos Pères"). The organization will save him from the defeat he has brought upon himself.

What has become of the suggestion of epic proportions in the third letter? It is here, for behind the principals there are fourth characters, a mass of shadowy figures, a conglomerate group, unified by doubt. Montalte speaks of the libertines, who seek only to doubt religion. The Jansenist evokes as examples to be faced the philosophers, the Epicureans, the idolaters, the atheists, the irreligious, and the unfaithful. It is as though Pascal were assembling the audience of the *Pensées*, all of these specific groups growing out of the indifferent ones, the neutral ones, of the third letter and even of the first.[4] Montalte joins more frankly now with the Jansenist and then even with the libertines in their right to doubt. One has to have the courage to face up, if one is to arrive at truth. Montalte looks through the Jesuit to the libertines, who are behind the scene.

The Jesuit is a comic figure not only through his own antics of tripping himself up, of tying himself in knots, but even more because of the contrast between him and the doubters. It is as though Montalte were saying to him: You take yourself seriously, but look through the

4. We note from the remarks in the third Preface of Wendrock Pascal's gradual realization of the uses of comic technique, the extent of the audience it could reach, and the preparation the writing of the *Provinciales* provided for the project of the *Pensées*. Wendrock pleads first his own careful authentication of facts: "Le dessein que j'avois de donner une version de ces Lettres m'ayant obligé de m'informer exactement . . . il m'est échappé peu de faits qui y aient quelque raport. Ce que j'ai donc appris par des personnes très-dignes de foi. . . . " The editor continues: "Alors Montalte qui n'avoit encore presque rien écrit, et qui ne connoissoit pas combien il étoit capable de réussir dans ces sortes d'ouvrages, dit qu'il concevoit à la verité comment il pouroit faire ce factum, mais que tout ce qu'il pouvoit promettre étoit d'en ébaucher un projet, en attendant qu'il se trouvât quelqu'un qui pût le polir, et le mettre en état de paroître. . . . Il vouloit le lendemain travailler au projet . . . mais au lieu d'une ébauche, il fit tout de suite la première Lettre, telle que nous l'avons. . . .

Cette Lettre eut tout le succès qu'on pouvoit desirer. Elle fut lue par les savans et par les ignorans. Elle produisit dans l'esprit de tous l'éfet qu'on en attendoit. Elle eut encore un autre éfet auquel on n'avoit point pensé. Elle fit connoître combien le genre d'écrire que Montalte avoit choisi étoit propre pour apliquer le monde à cette dispute. On vit qu'il forçoit en quelque sorte les plus insensibles et les plus indiférens à s'y intéresser; qu'il les remuoit, qu'il les gagnoit par le plaisir, et que, sans avoir pour fin de leur donner un vain divertissement, il les conduisoit agréablement à la connoissance de la verité" (third Preface, at Cologne, March 15, 1660, transl. by Mlle. de Joncoux, 1699)—Pascal, *Oeuvres*, G. E. ed., VII, pp. 66-67.

eyes of the neutrals, the libertines, those who are indifferent, and what kind of a figure do you cut? It is laughable. They know from experience ("de leur propre expérience"); they are realists. They will not stand for your playing with words; they know when you do not carry through on what you say, when you hedge, when you slide out from under, when you are self-serving. The dialogue with doubters in the *Pensées* produces the same comic view, as Pascal's own profound, recurrent doubt produces the same comic astonishment. He says to the Jesuit here and to the human being in the *Pensées*: You cannot pull the wool over people's eyes ("si vous n'êtes pas véritables en un article, vous êtes suspects en tous"). You cannot play the *dupeur* and expect to come out triumphant in the comedy. Hypocrisy will not do it. And when you make yourself believe in your charlatanry, there is no hope. The most zealous, says the Jansenist, act from motives they think are pure but realize afterwards are in self-interest ("sans qu'ils s'en aperçoivent quelquefois que longtemps après!").

Language.　The sublime and the ridiculous.

As the characters are set in juxtaposition, so the language of the letter, like the lines of caricature, becomes first a language of extremes. Irony expresses itself in oratorical exclamations in which elevated hopes are dashed on a mean reality: "que j'en vois de belles conséquences!" This is the cadence of frustration. It is lightened by the gushing language of the *précieuses*, "O que cela me plaît! . . . furieusement", mingled with the latin patter of the pedants, "J'appréhende furieusement le *distinguo*." The playing with words emphasizes hope that comes to nothing "like the sufficiency that does not suffice" ("semblable à cette *suffisance* qui ne suffit pas").

The bitterness of the conclusions that both sin and the
value of grace disappear does not lessen the comic
import in the rosy dream world of the Jesuit where
everyone is justified: "Béni soyez-vous, mon Père, qui
justifiez ainsi les gens!" Montalte delights in carrying
the consequences to their ultimate extremes, using
exaggeration to make incongruity stand out: If one
can manage not to think of God at all, all things become
pure for the future; hardened sinners have deceived the
devil by giving in to him; my friends never think of God
and they come out innocent as babes ("encore dans
l'innocence baptismale").

"Eh quoi!" is an exclamation of comic indignation. It
is followed here by "C'est une assez plaisante chose
d'être hérétique pour cela!" "Plaisante" is used now in
the fourth letter; it appears very frequently in the *Pensées*. Like the "étonné . . . étonnement" of the conclusion of the letter it is the language of astonishment, of
incongruity, of appearances, of fractured reality, like
a modernistic painting. Even the question that precedes
the exclamation with "plaisante" has the oratorical
value of an exclamation, as much as to say: "You cannot
mean it!"

We have noted the Jesuit's contemptuous "Ce sont des
rêveurs" and his later argument "après avoir un peu
rêvé". Let us not forget the delightful parrotting of the
Jesuit's "Je m'en vas bien vous convaincre" in the Jansenist's "Je m'en vas vous en éclaircir", with the emphasis on clarification rather than flimsy argument. It is
one example of the comic duelling grace and agility of
the conversation.

Words have a suggestive force for Pascal, projecting
his thought forward, not only in the Rabelaisian joy of
a sonorous proliferation of examples but to widen horizons, multiply evidences of incongruity, and create new

comedy. The word "libertines" carries him on to Epicureans, atheists, idolaters, unbelievers, infidels; and all who take joy in sinning, who are proud of it ("qui en font vanité"), especially aristocrats, line up to mock the Jesuit's facile enthusiasm. A new list of horrors comes to add itself to the lists of the third letter. The number is seven, which has not only biblical connotations but is one of the numbers traditional for luck in the game of chance. Avarice, indecency, blasphemy, the duel, vengeance, thefts, sacrilege, contrast with a shining trinity of chastity, humility, and "other Christian virtues". Aside from the enjoyment of the very thoroughness of the terms, these expressions point the way to comic incongruities in morality, in the following letter. Montalte cannot conceive of Epicureans praying when they consider it an insult to ask God for what we need, as if God were capable of amusing himself with thinking of us. Prayer becomes a mockery and evokes the image of a human comedy and laughing pagan gods.

Comedy of situation. The rubber dagger: the blade deflected.

The metaphor of the doctor and the cure, which recalls the Jansenist's parable of the second letter, has the same comic value of situation, in the human being helpless in the hands of these intermediaries of God for the very life of his soul, and the added laughable quality of distorted application of the parable. The lovers of pleasure, who find nothing wrong with themselves, are not looking for a doctor. It is all beside the point.

Theme.   The human comedy.

The theme of the human comedy is burgeoning in this letter. It begins with Montalte's "Beware of consequences" ("prenez garde, mon Père, aux dangereuses suites de votre maxime"). This warning will continue in the abuses in morality of the next letter, but meanwhile it requires a sketchy examination of all the ways of sinning, by surprise, by unawareness, by self-deception, all the "secret traps" ("pièges secrets") making the human being the dupe of circumstance, of absentmindedness, of narrowness of outlook, of covetousness. Thus the examination of custom, of justice, of vanity in the *Pensées*.

The Scriptural examples of inadvertent sin and the careful analysis of the quotation from Aristotle, apparently not taken from prompting notes of others[5], lead to the conclusion that there is no excuse in ignorance of good and evil.

In the face of the libertines' incredulity, the ultimate question surfaces, that religion is false, or that instruction is bad ("vous les obligerez à conclure, ou que la religion est fausse, ou du moins que vous en êtes mal instruits"). The *Provinciales* is the comedy of breaking through sham, of those who are badly instructed and have not the grace to know it. Through this portal one arrives at the new comedy of the human obliged to stumble forward in the game of the "Pari", blind and at the mercy of fate for the outcome, perhaps, but at least with the dignity of sincerity and acknowledged choice and will, for a throw of the dice, for involvement, for the courage to put himself on the line to win or lose.

---

5. "qui . . . ne semblent pas avoir été étudiés et signalés avant cette *Provinciale*"—*Oeuvres*, G. E. ed., IV, p. 232.

The Fifth *Provinciale*
High Comedy: The Happy Jesuit

In the fifth letter, with all the variety of techniques of comedy that he has already used, Pascal finds a new one (perhaps suggested by the Jesuit's inept quoting of M. Hallier's criticism in the fourth letter). With it he strikes a high level of humor from the second sentence of the introduction and maintains a heightening of effects all through the letter. With the quotations from their works and, by extension, with the remarks in the rapid dialogue of the main scene, Pascal puts the mockery, which might belong to Montalte, into the unfortunate mouths of the Jesuits in general and his Jesuit in particular. All of which allows the reader to indulge in an infinite sense of superiority, as he contemplates the strutting of these "men eminent in doctrine and wisdom, who are all led by divine wisdom". Pascal fosters this superiority: "You think . . . I am joking. I say it seriously, or rather it is they themselves who say it." As if with a wink that brings an answering smile, author and reader join in understanding.

Structure.   Unity of time, place, and action.

The initial technique determines the structure of the letter. The introduction, which is not long, is, for the first time, almost entirely a quotation. It is made-to-order comedy which Pascal could hardly have resisted once he saw it. Its position, strategically threaded through the first paragraph, marks the master touch in humor. As Pascal has noted in the *Pensées* (976): "La dernière chose qu'on trouve en faisant un ouvrage est de savoir celle qu'il faut mettre la première."

He launches into a preparatory interview with the Jansenist, at first secondhand, recounted by Montalte, and then with what is barely dialogue, almost monologue by the Jansenist, giving exposition and setting direction in a fairly composed manner. The tempo of the central and very developed scene between Montalte and the Jesuit is rapid, varied dialogue, agile, savory, full of verve. The antithesis in pace suits itself to the contrast in doctrines, one austere and aiming at simplicity, the other worldly and adaptable. The division also separates the conscious raillery in the interview with the Jansenist from the purest unconscious humor which the Father represents.

We have effectively a play in one act, where the lively main scene so carries the day that no real conclusion is necessary. The Jesuit himself announces the subject of the next letter, thus prolonging Pascal's original tone and technique. In his own inimitable way, the Jesuit sweeps himself into the new projected set of assertions designed to "edify", and Montalte is content to give him rope to do so. Montalte adds only a token send-off ("Voilà la fin . . . ") and a promise of high amusement to come ("vous serez satisfait") in order not to diminish the magnificent exit.

Characters.   The artistic triangle, the Jesuit at the apex.

The characters are specifically the three, Montalte, the Jansenist whom we have seen before, and the happy Jesuit, whose acquaintance we make here. Only the latter is backed this time by his whole troup of angels, eagles, phoenixes, who speak through the quotations from the

Jesuit casuists. They provide a three-dimensional heightening of the humorous effect in the comic figure. They also dominate the introduction and the scene with the Jansenist. Pascal fulfills his supposed promise to the Chevalier de Méré to deal with the casuists: "Laissez-moi faire. . . . "

Montalte is now a most accomplished master of ceremonies. He asks few questions of the Jansenist, just enough to keep the dialogue going, but they are the right questions, the critical ones, to get to the heart of the matter with no time wasted. It is useful to cede the field to the Jansenist for the necessary setting forth of the background and to hold in reserve his own lively character for the scene to come. He has already established his rapport with the audience (as surely as a Maurice Chevalier) in the introduction, with his quotation, "a society of men or rather of angels . . . foretold by Isaiah in the words, *Allez, anges prompts et légers*", and his question, "Is the prophecy not clear?", which invites the reader into the fellowship of laughing spirits.

He is prepared, wily, graceful. He seeks out a good casuist of the Society whom he had known and renews the acquaintance deliberately. He speaks with the irony of the disabused: "I admired them for the excellence of their politics", obviously not for their moral firmness or their sincerity. He manipulates and has no trouble getting his man on to the subject: "Comme j'étais instruit de la manière dont il faut les traiter, je n'eus pas de peine à le mettre en train." He is politely roundabout ("après quelques discours indifférents") and then, appropriately for the season (le 20 mars), asks to "learn" from the Father about fasting, "afin d'entrer insensiblement en matière". He is deft, deliberate, clever, in complete control of the situation, and he is an actor. He plays the part of the lukewarm catholic who finds it difficult to fast, complains at being urged to try hard. He plays with the Father and with the audience: "O que cela est divertissant!"

He expresses spurious admiration for all proofs offered, swallows everything (and what a gross dose it is!); yet he is always blandly to the point. To the Father's plea of relativity in morals, "c'est selon", he is quick to answer blankly, "Selon quoi?" He maneuvers, joyfully: "Je fus ravi de le voir tombé dans ce que je souhaitais." He fences with quick thrusts, at the same time inviting confession, to open his opponent's guard: Do you believe that? ("dites-moi, en conscience, êtes-vous dans ce sentiment-là?"). He backs his adversary into a corner: "What! because they put three lines in their books, one can look for chances to sin ('il sera devenu permis?')? I thought . . . the Scriptures. . . . " He leads him on: How to choose between opposite opinions, both rendered probable? ("On doit être bien embarrassé à choisir"). He pursues him: "If the other is more probable?" He never misses a weak point in the defense— has questions for every point. He can be silent, too, and that is the strongest attack of all; the opponent has exposed himself completely ("cela me fit pitié mais je ne lui en témoignait rien"). He can be droll and seem to draw back in mock alarm, even while he gets in his thrusts: "O mon Père! lui dis-je tout effrayé, tous ces gens-là étaient-ils chrétiens?" A last lunge puts the Jesuit right where he wants him for the next letter: there are a few obstacles ("trois ou quatre grands inconvénients"), Holy Scripture, the popes, the councils.

The Jansenist has his own dry humor: if the Jesuits do not intend to corrupt morals, neither do they concentrate on reforming them ("ils n'ont pas aussi pour unique but celui de les réformer"), for that would be bad politics. He says, doubtless with an urbane smile: "They have

a good enough opinion of themselves to believe that
it is useful and necessary for the good of religion that
they build their reputation everywhere and govern all
consciences." The restraint amounts to understatement
after the high-flown claims of the Jesuits, and is very
telling irony, by contrast. By providing both severe and
obliging confessors, the Jesuits manage to "keep all
their friends, and defend themselves against all their
enemies". This is a neat antithesis to the usual formula,
that one cannot please all the people all the time. The
Jansenist makes a brief, faintly supercilious remark
about the credulous and the lazy ("les simples, et ceux
qui n'approfondissent pas plus avant les choses") who
are content to accept these overall guarantees. He is
wryly disillusioned: the Jesuits in India and China sup-
press the "scandal" of the Cross if the people would not
credit a crucified God; or they permit idolatry, a figure
of Christ worn under the clothes. He opens the way for
Voltaire's vivid portrayal of Jesuits abroad. Anyone,
says the Jansenist scathingly, would always have enough
grace to live in piety "in the manner in which they understand it". Nature suffices to observe a morality which
is thoroughly pagan. With which sad shake of the head
he ushers his friend out. It is a reverse irony which states
reality in the light of disappointed idealism.

The Jesuit receives him and he is nothing if not magnanimous ("Il me fit d'abord mille caresses"). He offers
several reasons for dispensation from fasting until he
can find one that applies. He repairs to the library with
him for proof to further soothe any vestige of conscience
the absolved one might dredge up. No one who is sleep-
less after fasting has to fast, and no one has to change
the order of his meals, even if he can do so easily. He
offers the possibility of wine in the morning to Montalte
who does not need wine. One can drink it at any hour

and in great quantity, even the fortifying spiced wine *hypocras*, a detail which he hastens to note, since it had slipped his mind. He is delighted with Escobar's[1] allegory which inadvertently makes animals of Suarez, Vasquez, Molina, and Valentia. (Montalte gives the impression that he hardly has to lift a finger, that he can let the Jesuits do their own job of mocking themselves, with utter seriousness.) No one need fast between midnight and one o'clock if he will not be twenty-one until one o'clock. The Father does nothing but read Escobar night and day; he cannot tear himself away from such fascinating examples. There are other proofs: anyone who has tired himself from anything, like chasing after a girl, need not fast, even if he tired himself deliberately to avoid fasting. "Would you have believed it?" says the priest, taking the words out of Montalte's mouth.

To Montalte's mild suggestion that one might try to avoid occasions for sin, the Father has a jovial "Ho ho!" as if to say: "There I have you. You trapped yourself. Why, one might suffer inconvenience trying to avoid occasions. You did not think of that." And he has proofs for everything, extending Montalte's remark in the introduction that the texts themselves say it. One can even seek an opportunity to sin if it will do anyone any good spiritually. Asked if he believes what he is saying, he says no, but one can follow the principle because two other people believe it, and they are clever

1. Under the print of the portrait of Antoine Escobar (1589-1669), one finds the legend:

Ce casuiste débonnaire
Sur les maux des pecheurs versant l'huile et le miel
Par sa doctrine salutaire
Ouvre à tous les Chrétiens la grande porte du Ciel.

Exposition: Deux siècles de Jansénisme à travers les documents du Fonds Port-Royal d'Utrecht (16 janvier-18 mars 1974), Musée de l'Histoire de France.

people. If the word "clever" carries the necessary implication that it is all right if one can get away with it, the good Father seems unaware of that.

He shifts ground. When Montalte wants not the probable but the sure, the Father retreats to "You do not know what the doctrine is . . . I must instruct you . . . [in] the ABC's of our morality". Whereupon, he puts the burden on quotations.

He is engagingly unaware of his total disorientation with reality, with rationality, and is accordingly impervious to all Montalte's ironic comments. The members of the group are serious men ("savants"); therefore one can act on what they say. If they do not agree ("aussi sont-ils souvent de différents avis"), each can be trusted to make his opinion probable, even sure. No matter that one may be surer than the other. His *esprit de corps* is admirable. Anyone who has any other point of departure does not understand anything: "Vous ne savez pas ce que c'est. . . . Vous ne l'entendez pas. . . . Vous l'entendez bien peu." Even in mild reproach, gently chiding with finger-shaking or head-shaking: "I have noticed two or three times that you are not a good scholastic." ("J'ai bien reconnu. . . . ")

He is incurably modern, very proud not to quote any authority more than eighty years back, and he is tolerant, indeed modest, according to his lights. One does not have to be a Jesuit to have a probable opinion ("nous ne nous piquons pas d'honneur")—as long as one quotes us all the time, admiringly ("avec éloge"), like Diana, who calls the Order "le phénix des esprits". One finds oneself in the position of listening to a person all of whose opinions about himself are wrong.

Traditionalists are beyond the pale ("O bon Dieu! vous me faites souvenir de ces Jansénistes!"), and, condescendingly, the Church Fathers were good for their time.

His goodwill holds to the last—his good humor, and his moral astigmatism. The Holy Scripture, the popes, the councils? "Is that all? You frightened me. You think we would not have provided for that? . . . I should be very sorry ['marri'] to have you think us so lacking in our duty." His obtuseness keeps the audience constantly laughing with Montalte.

Meditation upon the sure comic effect of a character kept off base by a one directional attitude and imputing his faults to others is not lost in the *Pensées*. Classed under "Raison des effets", it becomes essential to the understanding of what man is in order to know where he should go. If the laugh is society's correctional gesture, what is wrong? Why does a lame man not irritate us and a lame spirit does? A lame mind says it is we who are lame ("D'où vient qu'un boiteux . . . ", 98). Then it is not the good-natured Jesuit we laugh at, but we, of the crippled minds, who do not know what we are and who avoid self-knowledge by blaming others. "Those who are on a ship think the ones who are on land are moving" (697). The comic frame remains, and we are the actors.

Behind the good-humored Jesuit of the letter stand first the casuists, whom he so happily accepts with their present danger of corruption, and then the Jesuit order shadowed in by the Jansenist. The doctrine of probable opinions, the source of the moral relaxation, is the means for spreading power. Easy, even imperative, absolution ("sur peine de péché mortel") at the sinner's convenience bends faith to fit the subject which ought to conform to it ("comme si c'était à la règle à se fléchir pour convenir au sujet qui doit lui être conforme"), as if "faith . . . were not one and invariable in all times and all places". So we have characters who manipulate the truth, who are hypocritical ("ils couvrent leur pru-

dence humaine et politique du prétexte d'une prudence
divine et chrétienne"), who act falsely, who play God,
mechanically making puppets of people. They are ruled
by their desire for dominance ("ils se sont répandus par
toute la terre"), which by implication, in the end, by
its abuse of truth, will defeat their purpose. One thinks
of the copy of Pascal's *Abrégé de la vie de Jésus-Christ*[2]
which has a page of Preface and then begins: "L'Eglise
a trois sortes d'ennemis, les Juifs qui n'ont jamais été de
son corps, les heretiques qui s'en sont retirez, et les
mauvais Chrétiens qui la déchirent au dedans."[3] The
characters sketched in by the Jansenist are machiavellian
rascals, creating a topsy-turvy world. They are the
dupeurs, who want to embrace everyone ("ils tendent
les bras à tout le monde").

In the *Pensées* Pascal concludes: "Je hais également
le bouffon et l'enflé [this sentence crossed out]. On ne
ferait son ami ni de l'un ne de l'autre" (610.)

Comedy of situation.   The merry-go-round.

In this garden of comic characters, comic situations
flourish. The Jesuit is happy with Montalte from one
end of the scene to the other ("Que vous êtes prompt!"),
notwithstanding some fatherly admonitions ("Vous ne
parlez pas proprement"). Montalte is constantly ironic,
and the audience is left wondering at every moment
whether the balance will hold. Will the irony get through?
Will the Father get angry? He never does, and each
new instance of audience uncertainty and renewed reas-
surance is more delightful than the last. The two characters continue so happy with each other, one really,

2. Archives d'Utrecht. "Le manuscrit original ayant été détruit
par Pascal, cette copie est le seul témoignage connu sur ce texte."
Exposition du Jansénisme, already mentioned.

3. *Pensées*, 858.

one falsely. The audience has the constant feeling of imbalance in the pit of the stomach that goes with the seesaw and that makes any child laugh.

The motion of our boat changes, and we go around in circles with our Jesuit pilot who has no pole for morality. One can look for an occasion to sin if the sinner's spiritual good or his neighbor's ("de nous ou de notre prochain") calls for it. Then what is spiritual good? What is benefit? What is sin?

Along with Montalte, we are in a dream situation. Nothing could be more fantastic. "Il me semble que je rêve quand j'entends des religieux parler de la sorte." We laugh with what Bergson has termed the relaxation of the necessity for common sense in a dream.

It is a magic world where one can brush away tradition: "O bon Dieu! You remind me of those Jansenists! You think Father Bauny and Bazile Ponce cannot [turn the trick and] make their opinion probable?" There is the key. Anything can be made to seem credible in this fairy-tale world. It is like prestidigitation with verisimilitude. A casuistic sleight of hand.

"You must not laugh." ("Il n'en faut pas rire.") This is said by the Jesuit with gentle seriousness to Montalte, but at the same time by Pascal to the reader as the surest way to make the reader laugh and to join with him in the best kind of comic relaxation.

And you must not think of opposing this doctrine ("ni penser combattre cette doctrine"). Even Montalte, with all his agility and purpose, cannot cut through these shimmering cobwebs, though he tries desperately: "I am not satisfied with the probable, I am looking for the sure." Frustration is complete.

One can transpose a rule for evidence for practical events into one for evidence in moral things ("des choses du monde à celles de la conscience"). Why not? If one serious man says it is so, it must be so, and Sanchez is a serious man.

You may follow the least probable opinion, although it is the least sure. The majority of our new authors say so.

Comedy of language and tone.   Crescendo and a bitter seed.

In this situation which is a reversal of all that is common sense, the comedy of language can reach its apex also in manifest nonsense. An abstract symbol can be transposed to the level of multiplication in numbers. Thus the metaphors of the introduction, quoted from the Jesuits, build from "angels" (not a lowly point of departure) to eagles, to "a troop of phoenixes", and on equally sound authority, since one (new) author has shown that there are several phoenixes ("un auteur ayant montré depuis peu . . . "). Like the repetition of a color in the opposite corner of a painting, the metaphor appears again near the end of the Jesuit's interview to underline and accentuate: Diana, an outsider, calls the Jesuit Vasquez "le phénix des esprits". The symmetry of art completes the caricature of the most extravagant pride.

The abrupt descent from the sublime to the ridiculous of the preceding letters is still with us in this introduction, the caricature in language made blacker by the situation. This time Pascal did not have to create the mock-heroic tone. The Jesuits wrote their own parody, even to stating: "They have changed the face of Christendom." Montalte answers with the double force of feigned agreement and ironic disillusionment: "Il faut le croire puisqu'ils le disent." In effect: "They have indeed."

The Jesuit's childish satisfaction in the beauty of

his accommodating texts comes through all the more rosily in the effusive language of the salon. Diana "a furieusement écrit", according to this Jesuit *précieux*. Everyone "loves" Escobar; he has such "pretty" questions ("Tout le monde l'aime. . . . Il fait de si jolies questions"). The reading is fascinating; it keeps one up nights. Montalte's tart acquiescence, "How diverting!" ("O que cela est divertissant!"), serves to add piquancy. The Father is "delighted" ("ravi") that Montalte finds it so, and Montalte is "delighted" ("ravi") to maneuver him into a desired position. Repetition is never a simple repetition but accentuates an effect by a reversal.

The whole letter hinges once again on a word totally divorced from its meaning. The Father is childishly happy, removed from any realistic concept of the word sin. Sin has lost all meaning, all whisked away by the magic wand of convenience. We answer what we please, or rather what pleases those who ask us ("ce qui plaît à ceux qui nous interrogent").

We arrive at this conviction by delicious stages. An opinion is probable if founded on some consideration. One serious doctor is sufficient to render an opinion probable. Because a serious man ("adonné particulièrement à l'étude") will not take a stand, unless he has a good and sufficient reason. To call this language gibberish would be to destroy the charm of the illogical circular logic. Transposed to dignified language, this is like a Lewis Carroll song made of real syllables or an A. A. Milne, Winnie-the-Pooh chant in syllables and words. These are real words. If one tries to see how they got into this order, one dissolves in a giggle. It is like the woman who said, "I don't like apples, and I am glad I don't like apples, because if I liked apples, I'd eat a lot of apples, and I don't like apples."

The uses of a list of names has provided treasure in style for great writers, and Pascal does not neglect this gold mine. The Old Testament has used them for dignity, Shakespeare for weight and poetic sonority, Rabelais for joy and enthusiasm, Victor Hugo for the luster of royalty. Pascal, both quoting and distorting, makes his choice for caricature. Deliberate enthusiasm, à la Rabelais, carries him to a total of forty-five. Grotesque combinations, Villabos, Conink, Ugolin, recall Voltaire's baron of Thunder-ten-tronckh. Awkward names, Bobadilla Simancha; a distortion of exoticism, Achokier; playful alliteration, Volfangi a Vorberg, Vosthery; parrotting repetition of a suffix from Fernandez to Sanchez combined with pretentious nobility from de Vechis to de Graphaeis; improbable combinations, Bizozeri, Dealkozer; syllables carrying connotations, Scophra; a surname twisted to improbablity by combination, Iribarne Binsfeld; tight, mincing, ridiculous sounds, de Pitigianis, Squilanti, Bisbe—all attest the suppleness, the virtuosity of Pascal's comic technique. There is no order in the arrangement for these proponents of a disordered morality. The consistent foreign flavor connotes barbarians beyond the pale ("Christians?" queries Montalte) to denote the "only ones by whom we govern Christendom today". Where are the French with their talent for rationality, for order?

Montalte's ironic exclamations take on many tones. The good word occurs as usual for the base reality ("O la bonne raison!") or the acrid "bien prudemment ordonné!" for required absolution. In reverse, the perception of reality is expressed for the unexpressed idealism: "Nous avons une belle liberté de conscience" and "Voilà de belles paroles . . . et pleines de consolation pour bien du monde." Clarity averred for obvious confusion in Montalte's ironic "Is not the prophecy clear?", concerning the Jesuit angels, is enhanced by serious, if foolish, repetition, "Cela n'est-il pas clair?" by the Jesuit, applied to the nonsense about the least probable and the least sure.

Restraint in expression, Montalte's disarming query, "sinon que c'étaient les sentiments de quelques particuliers", at the outset, only serves to emphasize the grotesque reality of the Jesuits' ambition, outlined by the Jansenist. The same understatement becomes ironic in his "Is one not obliged to avoid occasions for sin ('de les fuir')? That would be convenient enough" ("assez commode").

The reverse is exaggeration carrying implication to its farthest point in flippant, impertinent language: "One man can do anything he wants with people's consciences ("bouleverser les consciences à son gré")?

How discreet and restrained the use of Latin here to indicate the Jesuit's pedantry (not as in earlier letters) and deepened to carry other implications! The one sentence from Diana is the verse from Ovid,[4] translated by Pascal: "Si quelque dieu nous presse, un autre nous délivre." With its implication of multiple gods, the caricature takes on the bitter tone of the Jansenist's "leur morale est toute païenne".

The language of astonishment is constant. The Father's comical surprise ("Eh quoi? me dit le Père tout étonné") at the idea of any obstacles to his fine world of convenience ("de puissantes barrières qui s'opposeront à votre course") contrasts with Montalte's exclamations, sometimes bewildered, but often indignant. Montalte's expressions of stupefaction ("Eh quoi! . . . Mais quoi! . . . Quoi! . . . Quoi! . . . Eh quoi! . . . Quoi!") are more frequent than before and begin to be more definitely tinged with affliction.

4. *Tristes*, I, II, 4—*Oeuvres*, G. E. ed., IV, p. 314.

The epithet by which Pascal signals the incongruous and the laughable, which occurred once in the fourth letter ("C'est une assez plaisante chose"), appears twice here: "de si plaisantes choses. . . . La plaisante comparaison." The use of the word, carrying its many connotations, the laughable, the bizarre, the singular, the ridiculous, is gradually working up to its frequent appearance in the *Pensées*. One sees in this letter another term of astonishment, in the Jesuit's "Vraiment je vous admire. . . . " This, too, is usual language in the *Pensées* where the verb takes on many tones: I marvel, I wonder at, I am astonished that, I find it strange that.

The "si" and "tant" which indicated effusion and pretention in earlier letters change their color here. They reveal sad disillusionment in the Jansenist's observation: "the Christian virtues so unrecognized and so stripped of charity . . . so many crimes watered down, so many disorders tolerated."

The negative use of "étrange" shows the whole reversal of usual order, "that you will no longer find it strange" that all men can live in piety "as they understand it" ("de la manière qu'ils l'entendent").

In this most humorous of the letters, the bitter tone of the later ones begins to emerge. Baudelaire sees a common source for both reactions: "Le rire et les larmes . . . sont également les enfants de la peine. . . . "[5]

The other face of convenience in doctrine and convenience in sin is the simplicity, purity, severity, austerity of early Christianity. This is in part the contrast between the two scenes in the letter. The Jesuit himself says: " . . . l'esprit de la Société n'est pas celui de la sévérité chrétienne." What would be ironic in his opponent's mouth is all the more humorous for being serious coming from the Jesuit. The Jan-

5. *De l'essence du rire*, p. 978.

senist makes his stand clear: "c'est pour une vertu plus haute que celle des pharisiens et des plus sages du paganisme." It is what Strowski has called "le vrai sens de la vie chrétienne, le pur esprit de Saint Augustin et de M. de Saint-Cyran".[6]

Montalte is equally dissatisfied with the probable: "Je ne me contente pas du probable . . . je cherche le sûr." And Pascal notes, with a play on words, in the *Pensées*: "Mais est-il *probable* que la *probabilité* assure? Différence entre repos et sureté de conscience. Rien ne donne l'assurance que la vérité; rien ne donne le repos que la recherche sincère de la vérité" (599). As he widens the scope of his thought in the *Pensées* to include every soul, there is no need to abandon the detachment of comedy. The metaphor, the picture, changes, but the wonderment remains when he asks, "où prendrons-nous un port dans la morale?" (697). Laughter remains his right and comedy a legitimate perspective, in spite of Baudelaire's quotation: "Le sage ne rit qu'en tremblant."[7] To a degree the justification in the *Pensées* remains the same as in the words of Molière (reported by Racine) for the *Provinciales*: "Je vous demanderai . . . s'il faut renoncer à tout ce qui divertit, s'il faut pleurer à tout heure? . . . que dira le plaisant? Il voudra qu'il soit permis de rire quelquefois, quand ce ne serait que d'un jésuite; il vous prouvera que la raillerie est permise, que les Pères ont ri . . . les Lettres provinciales. . . . Le monde en a ri pendant quelque temps, et le plus austère janséniste aurait cru trahir la vérité que de ne pas en rire."[8]

6. Fortunat Strowski, *Pascal et sons temps. Histoire du sentiment religieux en France au XVIIᵉ siècle*, III, *Les Provinciales et Les Pensées* (Paris: Plon, 1928), p. 4.

7. *De l'essence du rire*, p. 976.

8. Racine, *Lettre aux deux apologistes de l'auteur des "Hérésies imaginaires"*, in *Oeuvres complètes* (Paris: Seuil, 1962), p. 313.

The Sixth *Provinciale*
The Jesuit Grown to Gigantic Proportions Overshadowing His World

Structure. Comic unity. A world taken over. Undisputed power.

The sixth letter, in structure, has the unity of one interview and the one central comic character. Except for a short introduction to announce the subject (the manner of reconciling casuistic doctrine with the popes, Councils, and Scriptures), to indicate exactness of quotations, and to aver the correctness of those in the preceding letter, Pascal launches immediately into the dialogue of the scene. The Jesuit speaks first and at length. The focus is complete, for though Montalte maintains his lively role, he uses it to throw the Jesuit into relief. Within this single scene the structure is clear and vivid, with concrete examples first to enliven general principles, a slight détente from action for theory, for exposition, and then the examples for the classes of people from top to bottom, providing dramatic scenes within the scene.

One is carried indeed to a third dimension, a circus ring within a ring in the tale of Jean d'Alba, who somehow executes a sort of revolution upon the Jesuits.

There is no closing, for the Jesuit acts until the very

last moment. He announces the subject of the next letter. Like a child savoring his dish, he keeps the best till last. The *gentilshommes* will be reserved for full treatment in another letter; it is, after all, to this class above others that adaptation of doctrine has to be made in this aristocratic worldly society.

Characters. The clown is king.

The characters are then Montalte and the Jesuit, with the Jesuit center stage. Yet this classic simplicity takes on a medieval richness, for the instant the Jesuit speaks, the parade of sinners begins before our eyes, vivid in the manner of the Old Testament and each with his drama to enact. There is musical-comedy adventure with fleeing assassins;[1] there are the wealthy parted with difficulty from their wealth, clergy, priests and monks, who recall the life of Villon, and valets, wily, miserable, beaten, and one way or another achieving their revenge upon their masters. The Jesuit suggests depth with an even richer cast of characters in one long sentence ("Nous avons donc des maximes pour toutes sortes de personnes . . . ") and adds merchants, poor people, pious women, other women, married people, everyone.

Montalte stimulates his speaker with his feigned admiration, which expresses itself in irony that chisels out clear, hard truth: "La loi de Dieu faisait des prévaricateurs . . . celle-ci fait qu'il n'y a presque que des innocents." He teases him with complete immunity, thereby joining with the audience to their delight: "I had

---

1. Pascal was having a fairly adventurous life himself, dodging the agents of the Jesuits who came across the street from their Collège de Clermont to the inn under the sign of the Roy David and nearly fell over the drying copies of the seventh or eighth letter without perceiving them, though one of the Jesuits sat next to the bed where the pages were spread out. *Oeuvres*, G. E. ed., VII, p. 62: "M. Perier aussitost alla en divertir M. Pascal, qui estoit dans la chambre au-dessus."

trouble finding a copy of Escobar. I do not know what has happened recently, to make it so that everyone is looking for one" ("j'eus de la peine . . . "). The audience, superior in their awareness of the success of the previous letter, enjoys the reference to current happenings.

As moderator, Montalte sums up what has been said and what is coming, injecting a surface orderliness which serves by antithesis to underline the utter confusion in the practices, and professing an openness which veils thinly his constant criticism: "il y en a pour le Clergé, la Noblesse, et le Tiers-Etat. Me voici bien disposé à les entendre."

Under his smooth transitions he laughs at his marionette. He nods in agreement: "Anyone has enough grace to strike such a bargain" ("tout le monde a des grâces suffisantes . . . "), pricking his opponent with the materialistic language that ought to make the expansive priest wary, but never does. Montalte objects, "the laws of the Church" ("il y a les lois de l'Eglise"), at once heightening the absurdity of the conclusions and sending them on their snowballing way. He stands before this semi-creation of his, struck dumb with the fantasy into which the enthusiastic Jesuit has projected himself: "Je fus si surpris de la bizarrerie de cette imagination, que je ne pus rien dire. . . . "

If Montalte points delightedly to the Jesuit, mocking him for having inadvertently entangled himself in a play on words ("on ne saurait trop estimer un si beau fruit de la double probabilité"), he expresses himself constantly at the same time in the disillusioned irony of a base reality wholly perceived: "Voilà . . . les ecclésiastiques bien à leur aise." If he maintains his detachment through the light touch of suggestion, the bitter truth lies underneath, deftly exposed to all eyes: "vos casuistes . . . y ont agi comme pour eux-mêmes."

The vaunted "charité" of the doctrine is a complete distortion of the Golden Rule.

Yet he keeps his comic stance to the end. Having turned the Father's own example of discontented valets against the Jesuits in the episode of Jean d'Alba, he soothes him down and then cannot resist indulging in his own play on words and his own flight of imagination. With malice he suggests even an extension of temporal power: "If on the one hand you are the judges of the confessors, are you not on the other hand the confessors of the judges? . . . oblige them to absolve the criminals who have a probable opinion, on pain of being excluded from the sacraments, so that probability will not lose face ('afin qu'il n'arrive point, au grand mépris et scandale de la probabilité') and your exculpated offenders be whipped and hanged." He proposes the increase in mischief to show the abysmal stupidity of his adversary who has not the wit to go the whole way. The Father's reaction keeps it in the realm of comedy, but the suggestion of inherent danger does not disappear, for a non-comic Jesuit is not known for his witlessness.

This Jesuit has his mania which is a boundless enthusiasm for the party, specifically for the new casuists. It takes genius ("c'est de qui n'appartient qu'aux grands hommes") to find probability in the opposite of the obvious. It takes an "ingenious and subtle" man: "Le Père Bauny y excelle." It is a pleasure to see this scholarly casuist find right on all sides ("Il y a plaisir de voir . . . "). The Father's enthusiasm runs to superlatives: "the subtlest of all the new methods, and . . . the finest point of probability." He is immensely proud of being modern: "one must not follow in morals the ancient Fathers, but the new casuists."

The so far off-center axis of his thought accounts for

his always missing the point. Valets cannot be absolved for transmitting dishonest messages if they consent to the sins of their masters, but they can be if they do it for their temporal convenience. If convenience is the measure for salvation, the Father is all right in his world, and all are absolved. He would never ask himself: "Why would a valet do it otherwise?"

He sees himself above all as a charitable, reasonable man. If one pays for an ecclesiastical title, with a motive which causes the beneficiary to give up the money rather than for the revenue-yielding charge itself, even though he expects the revenue, it is excusable. Who could refuse to admit such a motive? "No one is abandoned of God enough for that." It is wonderful to whisk simony out of existence. The ecclesiastics taken care of, the rest are all treated with equal consideration, "avec une pareille charité", from the greatest to the least, and he chooses valets first as the lowliest example.

The magnanimity that delights in seeing sin disappear results in a blind eye to obscenities. The Father is happy to indicate "un bel exemple" of favorable interpretation of papal edicts. That Montalte would be too horrified to report it does not occur to him, though the Father pointed it out for private reading. Montalte's calculated discretion (surely the most euphemistic form of burlesque) allows imagination to run riot, increasing the comic contradiction in the Jesuit's attitude, but Montalte means what he says, as Hermant's *Vérités académiques* attest: "S'ils fomentent le vice en promettant l'impunité, ils l'enseignent par les escrits qu'ils publient en langue vulgaire, de peur ce semble qu'il y ait quelqu'un parmi le peuple qui puisse ignorer les plus noires abominations . . . ils descendent aux dernieres particularitez; . . . ce qu'ont ignoré les Siecles les plus depravez du Paganisme, toutes les ordures, et toutes les saletez qui peuvent faire rougir l'effronterie mesme, se trouvent en abregé dans le livre d'un Jesuite."[2]

The Jesuit has his mannerisms of the pedant, using Latin to give weight to his statements. That he uses it to underline the wrong points, the most absurd, *probabiliter obligatus, et probabiliter deobligatus*, and lets Montalte catch him in the double probability, is all the more delicious. He allows himself a precious term: "qui le persécutait alors furieusement". He is a bit pompous, expansive as he holds forth, and unaccustomed to being disputed with: "Je vais vous expliquer . . . apprenez bien ceci . . . ne vous appris-je pas l'autre fois . . . ?" He has his testy, tactless moments: "Vous n'avez point de mémoire. . . . " With opposition he is quick to shift responsibility; if Montalte cannot stomach the idea that the Church approves all it has not specifically censured, that is Father Bauny's tenet: "Disputez . . . contre le Père Bauny." He lectures, point by point: "D'abord, le docteur *grave* . . . l'expose au monde. . . . Ainsi, en peu d'années . . . et, après un temps. . . . " He waxes biblical ("la jette comme une semence pour prendre racine") and proceeds with dignified rhythm to the peak of "cette grande maxime" which throws Montalte into confusion with its absurdity.

He holds forth with the greatest of pleasure and will brook no interruption. The astute suggestion from Montalte for enforcing power over the magistrates does not please him, though he grudgingly admits it is worth considering; since it was not his own idea, it cannot be of great importance. The story of Jean d'Alba he finds pointless ("Qu'est-ce que tout cela signifie?"). His own examples are fascinating, but he has no intention

2. Pascal, *Oeuvres*, G. E. ed., V, p. 9.

of wasting them on people who do not know enough
not to interrupt him ("je ne vous les apprendrai qu'à
la charge que vous ne me ferez plus d'histoires").

From his hired room at the inn under the sign of the
Roy David, opposite the Collège de Clermont,[3] Pascal
could watch the Jesuits' movements and gestures and
produce his composite caricature.

Driven by his particular distortion, the Father's
imagination can carry him all unwitting to such peaks
of absurdity that he becomes almost lovable. He means
well. One cannot oblige a priest to say mass every day,
according to the casuist, because he may have committed a mortal sin. On the other hand, if he has been
paid to say it every day, his sin is not the payer's fault;
consequently, the priest must perform the mass even
if he has just committed a mortal sin. On the Father's
own authority, if you did not let priests perform mass,
there would be fewer masses. It is obvious that many
masses so glorify God and so help human souls that it
is impossible not to agree with Father Callot that there
would not be too many priests if all men and women,
inanimate bodies and brute beasts were changed into
priests. A reader is left wondering for whom these
priests would say mass except themselves, to whom
they would be priests, and what human souls would
remain to be helped. All that, of course, is beside the
point, like Montalte's interruptions; the organization
is for the organization, even to the extinction of those
whom they supposedly serve.

In his unconscious mania, his primary trait as a comic
character is that he is totally devoid of a sense of humor
and, therefore, impervious to all irony. He will not be
put off his track by Montalte's little joke about copies
of Escobar being scarce; he ignores it ("Ce que je vous

3. Pascal, *Oeuvres*, G. E. ed., VII, p. 61.

disais, repartit le Père"). It seems incredible that he should be so dense as to miss the point about Jean d'Alba ("A quoi vous amusez-vous?"), but humor requires realism, and the Father is padded by an ivory tower insulation of theory ("Je vous parle des maximes de nos casuistes"), which inspires Montalte to ask, "Where were you then?" ("ne vous souvenez-vous plus de ce qui se passa en l'année 1647?") The Father answers with dignity: "I was teaching cases of conscience in one of our schools rather distant from Paris." Such moral isolation permits quite consistent good humor, shaded only by a childish irascibility about not being allowed to tell his stories without interruption ("vous m'interrompez par des histoires hors de propos").

The Jesuit is backed by the casuists he quotes, but he projects to them his ingenuous enthusiasm, so that general folly and stupidity take on his own character. That this is possible points to the evident danger. He is able to convince himself that the contradictions never existed: "ces contradictions prétendues".

His sinners are his flock to be given indulgent care. Since assassins are denied sanctuary, casuistry narrows assassins down by interpretation to paid assassins. Other assassins are not assassins; they are good people just helping their friends. The wealthy are obliged to give alms from what they do not need, but in practice almost no one has any excess, since one must improve one's condition; that takes care of kings as well. Obviously no one should be required to go through the eye of a needle. Pascal's note in the *Pensées*, 956, states the situation seriously: "Diana . . . Et ailleurs l'on n'est pas obligé de donner l'aumône de son superflu dans les communes nécessités des pauvres. Si le contraire était vrai il faudrait condamner la plupart des riches et de leurs confesseurs." In the letter, on the other hand, he assures comic effects on two counts. He maintains the absurdity in contrasting the theoretical and the practical so that his Jesuit remains removed from realism ("encore que l'affirmative [dans la question] fût véritable, il n'arrivera jamais, ou presque jamais, qu'elle oblige dans la pratique"), and he leaves the ridiculous words in the Jesuit's mouth.

A cleric must not leave off his habit, but conditions could be such that he might be caught in unsavory places, and naturally he would not want to cause scandal for the Order: better to leave it off.

Opposites cannot be true in the same sense, but both can be probable and, therefore, permitted. Besides, the Pope is in Rome and the casuists right here in France. Between opposites, choose what pleases most ("celui qui agrée le plus"). One casuist, "according to his whim" ("selon sa fantaisie"), Montalte notes wonderingly, can take care of any situation.[4] Those sworn to a life of fasting, like that of the faithful during Lent, do not have to fast. They might become bishops, and it would be inconvenient.

Since a monk finds it hardest of all to obey his superiors, he need not; he may hold a probable opinion different from his superior's, even if the superior is right. Chased out of his monastery, the monk is not obliged to correct his ways to go back.

Comedy of situation.   A world off its course.

The comedy of situation has multiple aspects and remarkable variety. With the Jesuit sketching his moral world, it is like being on the ocean with a pilot who makes the ship go around in circles. The examples of circular reasoning and illogical logic keep laughter bubbling constantly. With a sigh ("Hélas!") the Father

4. *Pensées*, 954: "Un seul dit vrai."

admits that they would like to keep strictly to the maxims of the Scriptures, but they are forced to adapt. People are so corrupt today. It is a case of Mohammed and the mountain ("ne pouvant les faire venir à nous, il faut bien que nous allions à eux"). If we did not condescend, "they might leave us, or worse, give themselves up entirely" to vice. One is left wondering what else this "condescension" encourages them to do.

The maxims must be so gentle that no one will be turned away, so as not to send anyone into despair ("ne rebuter qui que ce soit, pour ne pas désespérer le monde"). One opens one's eyes wide at the ingenuous priest. What surer road is there to despair? If there is no sure point from which to orient oneself, the seeds of despair are sown. This is the dilemma of the existentialists. It is also Pascal's question in the *Pensées* (with a metaphor which places a man in the comical position of being deceived by his senses): "Où prendrons-nous un port dans la morale?" (697).

The most piquant and complicated of the circular situations is Montalte's story of Jean d'Alba. Father Bauny maintains that valets, discontented with their wages, may steal from their masters, if they accepted their position out of need and if others make more than they do. Montalte comes through with a *conte*, heard in company and designed to amuse, on the order of Boccaccio's or Marguerite de Navarre's and naughty in its attack on priests. Pascal situates it immediately in the Jesuits' Collège de Clermont on the rue St. Jacques, which he overlooked from his hideout. The definition of a *correcteur des classes* ("servant vos Pères") was of a poor boy who whipped the pupils by order of the Jesuit regent or the prefect of classes.[5] Jean d'Alba was

5. Variant: "servant *de correcteur à.*" Definition of Richelet—Pascal, *Oeuvres*, G. E. ed., V, p. 48.

imprisoned by the Jesuits for the sin of stealing a few tin plates from them, which he had learned in his studies under a Jesuit was excusable. Nevertheless, he was convicted by a Jesuit who, in a deliciously thorough-going condemnation, declared the doctrine "illicite, pernicieuse et contraire à toutes les lois naturelles, divines et humaines, capables de renverser toutes les familles et d'autoriser tous ces vols domestiques". Thus a boy who is paid too little for whipping pupils has the frustration of being whipped for what he has learned is pardonable from those who whip him. A Jesuit judge condemns what the Jesuits advance as doctrine, but has the boy whipped anyhow and the pages containing the maxims burned by the same hand ("bourreau") at the same time, and the Jesuits who brought the accusation are never to teach the doctrine, on pain of death ("sur peine de la vie"). All of this is turned against our ivory tower Jesuit, who cannot see that it applies to him and who was somewhere else at the time, teaching about consciences.

That this Jesuit draws a general laugh is not the only triumph of the valets. They can carry letters and presents, help their masters climb ladders to get in windows, hold the ladders, though holding a ladder in itself is rather dangerous, and get paid for all this with a good conscience; they have learned from Father Bauny to perform all these duties "innocently" for their masters. Valets are figures of comedy (Marivaux, Beaumarchais), especially when they serve to show up their debauched lords.

The Jesuit does manage temporary triumphs. If he has to turn women, animals, and stones into priests to do it, he does momentarily shut up his questioner with all the latter's bothersome objections so that he can continue unimpeded ("de sorte qu'il continua ainsi").

The ambiguity of the whole situation keeps the audience continually on the verge of laughter. The Jesuit is always serious ("Voyez-vous combien cela est judicieux"). Montalte, answering with apparent respect, is always thinking the opposite, meaning the opposite ("Je n'attendais rien moins de 24 Jésuites"). The audience can never be quite sure the balance will hold, and then, improbably, it does.

Comedy of language. The quicksands of dependence on words.

The humorous uses of language are subtle and varied, to underline a jovial but dangerous absurdity. The terms of Biblical parables ("la jette comme une semence pour prendre racine") are a reverse application of dignified language to cover a shady meaning, not the firm ground of truth. The stately cadences of the passage build to the insidious conclusion that a probable opinion of a serious man ("un docteur grave"), if not opposed, is tacitly approved by the Church. So the discreet use of Latin to lend authenticity and dignity to ridiculous practices and reasoning becomes pretentious language heightening the effect of absurdity.

The Father sees nothing funny in speaking of Valentia as one of the four animals of Escobar, referring to the allegory of the fifth letter. He sees only the untouchable dignity of the profession which is armor enough even against making a man into an animal.

A game of numbers can substitute for integrity. A priest can be paid more than once for the same mass; he can accept the payment as for a third of a mass. Montalte's objection is that he cannot sell his own benefit from the mass. The material and spiritual levels are not interchangeable. And Montalte parrots the Jesuit's meaningless phrase: "If I were a serious man I could make that probable" ("pour peu que je fusse *grave*, je rendrais cette opinion probable").

The absurd contrast of extremes, for the most frequent crimes the most gentle maxims ("les vices auxquels on est le plus porté . . . des maximes si douces") leads to the slippery conclusion, hazardous through its practical grain of truth: the laws of the Church lose their force when they are no longer observed. The double perspective on this statement by the Jesuit who makes it, and through Montalte's eyes, provides very compact, condensed comic effect.

With the doctrine of probability as the essence of the difficulty, the word "probably" lends itself to comedy as an out for everything. The Jesuit entangles himself in these uncertainties. The monk who must supposedly obey his superior, who may be right, but not right in every point and in every way, is only probably held to obedience and is probably not held to it at all.[6]

Montalte's two-edged reaction is all contained in the word "comme". "Vos casuistes . . . y ont agi comme pour eux-mêmes." It contains the Jesuit's firm impression of his own charitableness and the illusion in the distortion of the Golden Rule.

Montalte's beautifully balanced reversal of terms at the end of the letter, "If you are the judges of the confessors, you are also the confessors of the judges", with its dangerous suggestion under a teasing wit, has the bitter humor of Pascal's note in the *Pensées*: "Au lieu de Dieu la grâce pour y aller" (954).

---

6. Pascal has developed the comedy of situation and language in the letter far beyond the note in the *Pensées*: "Probable. Quand il serait vrai que les auteurs graves et les raisons suffiraient je dis qu'ils ne sont ni graves ni raisonnables" (722).

Part Two

Humor in the *Pensées*

Preview of Techniques and Procedures in Humor in the *Pensées*

The techniques applied by Pascal intertwine with great and subtle variation, following the convolutions of his thought. Aside from this foremention and the commentary on individual texts, it would seem artificial and arbitrary to tear a study of style apart from his thought, given his attitude that style should be so much a part of the man himself that it would not make itself felt except in its effectiveness and that it should in all instances subjugate itself to his main aim as a true art of persuasion.

Destructive wit.

Wit has its special uses for attacking and destroying, all of them essential to Pascal for stressing the necessity for humility. The gentlest wit is a teasing, laughing tone, but penetrating, nevertheless, to prick man's vanity by exposing the inadvertent revealing of individual idiosyncracy, human blindness, narrowness, prejudice.[1] A wry, grudging humor turns in upon movements of charity to expose pride and self-indulgence. This merges to ironic diminution, to belittle man's capacity for charity, self-denial, sincerity.[2] Elsewhere

1. See p. 153.
2. P. 116.

it diminishes apparent social order to a matter of chance.[3] The grotesque, by an article of clothing or by an incongruous detail of physical characteristic or grooming, reduces and burlesques, by caricature, the proud or pompous.[4] Indeed, Pascal generalizes on this procedure, using the technical language of comedy as a parallel for the "mask" of appearances.[5] Raillery, through metaphor, as well as direct invective, sketches the world as an "hôpital de fous", to humiliate those who think themselves kings and emperors.[6] We see even a kind of inverted humor, since humor requires that man place himself above himself to attack his own vanity so that the manner of perception constantly negates its own conclusion, revealing the vicious circle of man's pride in his own humility.[7]

Scornful irony assaults the lethargy of man who does not recognize his disoriented state.[8] Heavy sarcasm lashes at what Pascal sees as pretentious and deliberate superficiality in Montaigne.[9] Heavier sarcasm and invective direct themselves toward hypocrisy in human laws. Bitter, castigating satire, in the tone of righteous indignation,[10] against the shallowness of diversion for man, the dethroned king, changes to a kind of pitying humor for *un roi dépossédé*.[11]

The bitterest tone of all reflects, on a cosmic scale, the humorous value of frustration before the fact of death, the absurd human condition, the gigantic frus-

3. Pp. 140-141.
4. Pp. 118, 148, 149.
5. Pp. 149-150.
6. P. 118.
7. Pp. 121-122.
8. P. 129.
9. Pp. 125-126.
10. P. 157.
11. P. 158.

tration implicit in the eternal mystery of existence.[12]

Thus this destructive wit is distilled in metaphor, teasing, irony, raillery, sarcasm, and satirical invective in a detached, humorous, often pitiless view of humans to awaken one to the search for betterment, for honesty, for improvement, for spirituality.[13]

Persuasive, attractive wit.

To make such destructive humor palatable, acceptable, even pleasurable, and therefore persuasive, other tones and techniques are required for artistic comedy.

There is the gentle, winsome humor of the *honnête homme*, graceful, appealing, delicate, courteous, which uses the first person in an example on vanity[14] or expresses an attack in general terms, specifically to diminish praise of himself.[15] It is this personal adoption of the stance of universality, as well as objective generalization, that brings a note of compassion into his humor and an attitude of charity.[16] The beauty,[17] elegance, and purity of his style, to be noted particularly in connection with his use of metaphor, make for a powerful artistic element of persuasion.

Equally important is the fun of dramatic humor, the value of surprise, the unexpected, successive surprises in the scenes Pascal flashes before us,[18] achieved sometimes by color, concrete detail, or structure of the sentence.[19] Synthetic, dynamic use of drama of movement, of scene and shift, enlarges the scope and

12. P. 136.
13. Pp. 129-130.
14. P. 124.
15. P. 116.
16. P. 116.
17. P. 117.
18. P. 119.
19. P. 149.

horizon of surging thought.[20]

Not to be neglected is the subtle flattery of the reader in the comic approach, based upon a previously accepted rapport assuming a common ground of good sense as a measure of things. A similar rapport is implicit in the satirical paradox, where hope is necessarily attached to the objectivity of humor, for humor, which is intellectual, is based on faith without which intellect cannot operate.[21]

Techniques in style for humorous effect.

The unexpected, the incongruous, the value of surprise is achieved often by syntax. Lighthearted verbs contrast with their serious subject to describe the antics of the philosophers, to lighten the scene, to make it amusing.[22] An adjective linked with a noun expresses irony by an obvious, irrational juxtaposition of opposites: "plusieurs [principes] *excellents* du *faux.*"[23] The antithesis of adjective and verb, then verb and adverb, in successive small shocks gives agreeable little ironic jolts: "un *merveilleux* instrument pour nous *crever* les yeux *agréablement.*"[24] An adjective obviously contradicts the meaning of its noun ("Plaisante justice") for an effect of rhetorical irony.[25] The mocking adjective pleases him: "Plaisante raison"[26] and "la plus plaisante cause de ses erreurs" (*Pensées*, 44). An adverbial phrase introduces an element of doubt, essential to the movement of thought, in the midst of a straightforward statement: "Le hasard, en apparence, fut la cause. . . ."[27]

20. Pp. 128-129.
21. Pp. 119-120.
22. P. 118.
23. P. 126.
24. P. 135.
25. P. 142.
26. P. 126.
27. P. 146.

The surprise of a phrase in apposition at the end of a statement negates its whole positive effect, forcing thought: "le motif [d'être heureux] . . . de tous les hommes, jusqu'à ceux qui vont se pendre. . . . "[28] A noun denoting disorder, well chosen for denigration, set against a verb expressing order, produces irony: "pour *régler* un hôpital de *fous.*"[29] The satire in a curriculum for education depends upon the humor of a rhetorical question which casts the final and definite shadow of doubt upon the whole.[30]

Choice of vocabulary, derogatory terms in common use (*fous, coquins*) make an imagined conversation amusing.[31]

Humorous hyperbole heightens the effect of the fearful philosopher on a plank over a precipice.[32]

A touch of burlesque, of the grotesque, makes a preacher humanly comical and a grave magistrate vulnerable to frivolous reactions.[33]

Onomatopeia lends a sentence the rhythm of the dance, emphasizing the concentration of the dancer to caricature superficiality of attitude with this light rhythm.[34]

Metaphor contributes to comic effect by its density and conciseness. The world is an "hôpital de fous",[35] and the disparagement goes further: "les fous . . . pensaient être rois et empereurs."[36] The comparison of the perspective of those who are on land and those who are in a ship leads to the compact metaphor "un

28. P.138.
29. P.118.
30. P.151.
31. P.141.
32. P.127.
33. P.148.
34. P.156.
35. P.118.
36. P.118.

port dans la morale"[37] to disparage vividly self-deception by appearances and consequent frustration. A deft metaphor ironically disposes of the philosophy of Descartes as the "romance of Nature", a novel like *Don Quixote*. There is immense irony in the very poetic image of man, *le roseau*.[38] As much beauty and as much ironic frustration, as well as hope, reside in the lovely and incisive metaphor of the waking state of man as "un autre sommeil" in the context of immortality,[39] for doubt diminishes the possibility of relying upon one's own impressions. Frustration is implicit even in the power of Pascal's art to persuade the reader, through the poetry of style and metaphor, to an unpalatable and logical conclusion: "nous n'avons aucune idée du vrai."[40] Ironic contradiction on order in writing[41] and on symmetry[42] tend to disparage basic principles of art,[43] to temper admiration for art, and more profoundly, to indicate the finite quality in human creativeness, the danger of art as another kind of "appearance".[44] This presents a frustrating conclusion for the artist as a creator, a satirical paradox in itself. The passage that gives us the comedy of the magistrates[45] makes comedy itself, with its "grimace", into a metaphor which is the mask of truth.

Personification has multiple comic uses: apparently to ridicule capriciousness in nature, la "répugnance de la nature pour le vide", but actually to disparage a

37. P.122.
38. P.126.
39. P.128.
40. P.128.
41. P.152.
42. P.154.
43. P.154.
44. P.152.
45. Pp.149,151.

scientist for illogical application of such a conception;[46] to ridicule caprice and rashness through the figure of chance, the sower: "la témérité du hasard qui a semé les lois humaines".[47]

Antithesis is central and essential to Pascal's presentation of ideas, as a symbol of a shock of ironically opposing concepts that thrust one into new thought and larger perception, as in the dynamic absurdity of the small cause and the large effect in history.[48] Sometimes, this can be a paralleling of simple with pompous language to show obvious superfluity.[49] More characteristically, it is often the ironic contrast of two levels, the concrete or practical and the abstract or spiritual: the absurdity of choice of occupation by custom, not nature;[50] laws made according to geographical boundaries, not justice;[51] royal succession by birth, not virtue;[52] use of violence, physical force, not justice.[53]

Frequently, this same contrast of levels comes subtly through two meanings of one word: les gentilshommes, as a practical division of classes or to indicate true nobility;[54] the honnête homme, product of seventeenth-century education or the more universal, and basic, spiritual concept of the honnête homme;[55] what should be "first" in the order of writing a book or what is "first" in importance,[56] an effect achieved by humorous inver-

46. P.126.
47. P.143.
48. P.131.
49. P.153.
50. P.141.
51. P.142.
52. Pp.143-144.
53. P.144.
54. P.145.
55. P.150.
56. P.152.

sion of the sentence: "la dernière chose . . . est . . . la
première."

The most fundamental antithesis depends on comedy
by theme, the ironic opposition of all forms of diversion
to the basic questions of existence.[57]

Constructive humor.

In all of these aspects of humorous expression, the
efficacy of truth is implied.[58] Comedy is useful, humiliation is salutary, the facing of oneself is preliminary to
salvation. This is achieved through the distance implicit
in objectivity. Like the *"figures"* of the Old Testament,
the distortions of comedy present by their adverse face
a prefiguration of truth. Flux and impermanence in
human love, humorously expressed,[59] the mingled good
and evil in the institution of marriage,[60] examination
of the self,[61] areas in which one takes oneself very
seriously and finds oneself absurdly frustrated, bear
the implication of the concept of divine love, charity,
the realm of *le coeur*. This is the eventual satirical paradox. The levels of frustration, like the levels of metaphor
within metaphor,[62] express, in ever widening circles,
the unity of existence. Comedy becomes the symbol
of the unending search, through appearance, for freedom
in truth which gives the lie to appearances or redeems
them as a foreshadowing.

57. P. 151.
58. P. 116.
59. P. 133.
60. P. 133.
61. Pp. 133-134.
62. Pp. 138-139.

Importance of the Comic Vision

Out of the deep feeling of alienation and the inevitable sense of flux in our fast moving modern age, the courage to move forward creatively must find a point of departure. For the perspective that Pascal strove to achieve humor was apparently essential.

It is no accident that French classicism finds profound expression and worldwide reputation in three geniuses so different in attitude as Molière, La Fontaine, and Pascal. Molière creates comedy often approaching the tragic; La Fontaine makes of the fable a dramatically humorous, flexible metaphor; and Pascal writes in prose that is dramatic, satirical, poetic, in the *Pensées*, although he is directly serious on the subject of the proofs of the Christian religion. Even then he draws his arguments from images (as he does in humor), the "figures", the prefigurations of the Old Testament to prove the truth of the New.

As the human being sees only in part, truth must be glimpsed through appearances, and appearances, already a distorted image of truth, carry with them the element of the incongruous.[1] The *Provincial Letters* are only a preparation and an approach to the subtlety of the use of the comic vision in the *Pensées*. In the true classical manner, the particular, distorted, ludicrous, is used to prove the universal and the true. The latter is stated

1. John M. Alcorn, "Sight and Satire; The Quality of Vision in the Writings of Molière, Pascal, and Swift" (Deposited Harvard University Library, June 18, 1951), p. 10.

directly only occasionally and with much repetition
and similarity in form,[2] while the distorted comic vision
is clothed in variety of image, attractive and diverting.[3]
Mr. Weber sees Montalte in the *Provinciales* as a "living
contact between truth and falsehood" in the search for
a key to Pascal's complex vision.[4] It is our purpose here
to study the comic approach for the profoundly serious
purpose of the *Apologie*, in which Pascal reaches the
full mastery of his powers.

In such a work, attack through comedy implies idealism and a degree of optimism. One does not take the
trouble to ridicule if there is no conception of a better
state of affairs or no hope of achieving any improvement. Detachment and impersonality in humor (as
contrasted with the individual involvement of the tragic
approach) is essential to the objectivity of classicism
(as well as the sanity of humans), and Pascal in the most
serious of his works does not in any way relinquish the
literary attitude and language for which he showed such
aptitude in the *Provinciales*. This lively, varied, glancing
stance illuminates the paradox of the misery and greatness of the human being held up to the screen of truth.

Critics are diverse in their opinions. M. Guardini sees
no humor at all in Pascal, nor in his family: "And Pascal
lacks one more thing [besides an appreciation of nature
and art!]: Humor. We know no passage which would

2. " . . . L'homme . . . doit souhaiter après avoir ainsi connu
ce qu'il est, de connaître aussi d'où il vient et ce qu'il doit devenir"—
Etienne Périer, Preface to Port-Royal edition of the *Pensées* (Pascal,
Oeuvres complètes, p. 495).

3. "Pascal a le sentiment que nous ne percevons pas la vérité
directement mais par la négation de sa négation"—Jean Guitton, *Génie
de Pascal* (Paris: Aubier, 1962), p. 97.

4. Joseph Weber, "Person as Figure of Ambiguity and Resolution
in Pascal," *PMLA*, vol. 84, no. 2 (March, 1969), 317.

reveal even a tinge of it."[5] He admits to satire in the *Provinciales* but will not recognize it as humor because it is "sharp" and "biting".

Mr. Mortimer finds no difficulty in noting Jacqueline's "compassionate humor" at Pascal's visits to her for guidance: " . . . elles furent si fréquentes et si longues que je pensais n'avoir plus d'autre ouvrage à faire."[6] He mentions the "sedate humour which distinguished all that family" (p. 20). He notes in the *Provinciales* a daring "hilarity" (p. 126), "delicate satire", "humorous relief", a "sense of fun" in the picture of the Jesuit Father (p. 149), "irrelevance which is one hallmark of humour" (p. 138) in the *Réponse du Provincial aux deux premières lettres de son ami*. He does not neglect (p. 118) Pascal's letter to Fermat in Toulouse, when algebra confirmed the answer geometry had given: "Je vois bien que la vérité est la même à Toulouse et à Paris." The humor is clear when Pascal chooses as an address, to avoid recognition, the inn opposite the Jesuit school (p. 140).

M. Baudouin accepts readily Jacqueline's gentle humor (in the letter of December 1, 1655) when she protests her brother's wishing to dispense, as much as possible, with "superfluous" household implements and the services of domestics in the latter stages of his devotion and dedication: " . . . vous mettez des balais au rang des meubles superflus . . . il vous sera glorieux et édifiant aux autres de vous voir dans l'ordure, s'il est vrai, toutefois, que ce soit le plus parfait. . . . "[7] In commenting upon the "rire agressif" of the *Provinciales*,

5. Romano Guardini, *Pascal for Our Time*, tr. Brian Thompson (New York: Herder and Herder, 1966; Orig. ed., München, 1962), p. 211.

6. Ernest Mortimer, *Blaise Pascal, the Life and Work of a Realist* (London: Methuen, 1959), p. 122. Letter of Jan. 25, 1655.

7. Charles Baudouin, *Blaise Pascal ou l'ordre du coeur* (Paris: Plon, 1962), p. 147; *Oeuvres*, Pléiade ed., p. 1377.

he invokes the names of Molière and Voltaire,[8] admits for this work "toutes les nuances dans la combinaison du rire et de la colère", and cites, with Pascal, Tertullien: "Rien n'est plus dû à la vanité que la risée; et c'est proprement à la vérité qu'il appartient de rire parce qu'elle est gaie, et de se jouer de ses ennemis, parce qu'elle est assurée de la victoire" (Onzième lettre).[9] Yet he assumes that with the termination of the Lettres Pascal breaks clean with the comic vision ("Le temps de rire est passé") and, indeed, has not time to laugh: "D'autant plus que Pascal se trouvera aux prises, définitivement, avec la souffrance et la faiblesse extrême du corps, et que le temps va lui manquer."[10] When did Pascal renounce any aspects of his vision? All are useful. As for his physical suffering, it was not new, and Gilberte, in this period of great charitable acts of Pascal, showed him capable of answering with wry humor to protests against excessive generosity: "J'ai remarqué, que quelque pauvre que l'on soit on laisse toujours quelque chose en mourant."[11]

In fact, the new tone of la charité that marks the Pensées as quite apart from the Provinciales in no way precludes humor. In the Onzième lettre Pascal announces the transition in tone between the two works: " . . . on peut rire des erreurs sans blesser la bienséance. Et je vous dirai aussi, mes Pères, qu'on peut rire sans blesser la charité," using as his authority the quotation from St. Augustine: "la charité oblige quelquefois à rire des erreurs des hommes, pour les porter eux-mêmes à en rire et à les fuir." If this note of la charité is rather lacking in the Provinciales, as the reaction of his adversaries

8. Ibid., p. 81.
9. Ibid., p. 83; Provinciales, p. 420.
10. Ibid., p. 85.
11. Vie par Mme Périer, Oeuvres, p. 27.

reflects ("quoique ce soit une des choses que vous me reprochez dans vos écrits"), the realization of a more perfect use of humor eventually gains ascendancy in Pascal's mind. Is it not a truer, more objective, more detached humor that includes a charitable attitude? Is it not a higher, more universal humor that can attenuate the immediate sting of attack by ranging oneself along with all men in the ludicrous state of self-deception? Pascal retains the grace, elegance, and appeal of *l'honnête homme* preeminently in the *Pensées*.[12] Mr. Slights recognizes the mask of *honnêteté*, restraint and magnanimity, in the Fourth to the Tenth *Lettres provinciales*. A true tone of *honnêteté* comes through in the *Pensées*.[13]

Humor in the *Pensées* is both constructive and compassionate. For that reason this work speaks more directly to us. That is the true *art comique de persuader*. By humor, and delicacy, and beauty of form he leads us to otherwise unacceptable humiliation, but a humiliation in its true sense salutary, a facing of self without which it is impossible to save oneself or be saved.

He would not, in speaking to the libertine and to the evasive element in the thinking of all humans, give up this language the sophisticated understand so well and which he himself had learned so readily in his "worldly period", nor would he make the mistake of his sister Gilberte, who called it "le temps de sa vie le plus mal employé".[14] A man who could use misery to

12. Is it not the essence of Molière's universal appeal that he accepts and loves his characters even as he ridicules them, that each character is given his due time in the center of the stage? It is symbolic, as well as fact, that Molière acted in his own plays.

13. William W. E. Slights, "Pattern and *Persona* in Pascal's *Lettres provinciales*", *Kentucky Romance Quarterly*, 14 (1967), 137.

14. Though she recognizes his talent for the worldly tone: "Il est vrai que, quand il parlait du monde il en développait si bien tous les ressorts

prove greatness, or illness to produce saintliness, would not lose sight of the value of the apparently light or frivolous to turn a human to the most serious considerations of existence. He did not hesitate to use *le pari* in the language of roulette as an argument for faith.

He justifies his approach with precedent on a very high level of intellectual investigation: "On ne s'imagine Platon et Aristote qu'avec de grandes robes de pédants. C'étaient des gens honnêtes et, comme les autres, riant avec leurs amis" (*Pensées*, 533). The expression, "grandes robes de pédants" caricatures, not the philosophers, but the reader who visualizes them so and distorts them. Might one say that this is sometimes also the error of the readers of the *Pensées*?

The philosophers, in this *pensée*, adopt the dramatic attitude of Hamlet (life is a stage), and the immediate comic effect is in the unexpected, incongruous, suggestive force of the verbs: "Et quand ils se sont divertis à faire leurs *Lois* et leurs *Politiques*, ils l'ont fait en se jouant. C'était la partie la moins philosophe et la moins sérieuse de leur vie; la plus philosophe était de vivre simplement et tranquillement. S'ils ont écrit de politique, c'était comme pour régler un hôpital de fous." The reader laughs, feeling his own superiority, however false. Pascal at once destroys the feasibility of false superiority: "Et s'ils ont fait semblant d'en parler comme d'une grande chose, c'est qu'ils savaient que les fous à qui ils parlaient pensaient être rois et empereurs. Ils entrent dans leurs principes pour modérer leur folie au moins mal qu'il se peut" (533).

As with Hamlet, the human being becomes a player,

---

qu'il était aisé de concevoir qu'il était très capable de les remuer et de se porter à toutes les choses qu'il fallait faire pour s'y accommoder . . . "—*Vie*, p. 21.

grotesque, foolish. The players present a metaphor within a metaphor. First scene: the philosophers, their dignity made grotesque, playful. Second scene: the image of the human being superimposed, the setting more comprehensive, *un hôpital de fous*, the philosophers representing the doctors, making man more grotesque and foolish, because they are deliberate, knowing, and therefore restored (only moderately) to their position of dignity. Plot: surprise upon surprise, reversal after reversal. Epilogue: a scene in itself with the human in a new role, the fool playing the king. A classic comedy, on Pascal's scale, presenting in a few lines the position in the universe, man in his misery, diverting, full of antics.

The humorous, the satirical, is the language which challenges preconceived ideas, accepted impressions, contradictions taken for granted and, therefore, not examined.

Its appeal lies in its quality of courage. The social grace of humor is for those who know the depth of their misery and that of others, who can look pleasantly at others, taking account of their brotherhood in sadness, and beguile them into the necessary objectivity, saying in effect, "Come, let us see what can be done."

Before action one must fasten upon reality. If the whole theater of Molière is directed toward examining and laughing at foibles on the human and social plane, Pascal carries his perspective to a different depth with cosmic reach so that humor becomes the language of his whole intellectual challenge.[15] It is the objective language of the detached and rational approach, the *esprit de géométrie*. Humor assumes rapport with the

15. "Le comique exige . . . ,pour produire tout son effet, quelque chose comme une anesthésie momentanée du coeur. Il s'adresse à l'intelligence pure"—Bergson, *Oeuvres*, p. 389.

reader or audience on the basis of common sense. Good sense depends upon reason. Courage and satirical paradox are inherent in the faith which is the point of departure for mathematics with all its implications, foreseen in Pascal, realized in the relativity of Einstein.[16]

For a sincere question of the existence of God and the efficacy of faith in Christ, Pascal must challenge his worldly reader first on the level only of reason, of common sense. Curious that the language of good sense so often becomes humor and that the language itself is as illusive in its nature as the deceptive appearances, attractive and destructive, which it incisively caricatures and throws into cutting relief, and as the basic problems philosophers attack. Bergson has commented on the indefinable source of laughter, citing predecessors as illustrious as those used for justification by Pascal.[17]

Pascal characteristically abandons neither the social advantage nor the cosmic implications of humor. Persuasion demands eloquence, and eloquence requires a pleasant approach for the worldly, though there must be in it nothing false: "Eloquence. Il faut de l'agréable et du réel; mais il faut que cet agréable soit lui-même pris du vrai" (*Pensées*, 667).

Critics seek a "key" to Pascal's thought. Edgeless, he escapes the limits of the "keys".[18] None seem to

16. "C'est l'éclatement de toute rationalité de l'univers qui se cache sous la victoire de nos mathématiques. Que le vrai débat soit là apparaît dans l'attachement même d'Einstein à une rationalité en soi du monde—son angoisse la plus profonde venait de la sentir menacée"—Manuel de Diéguez, *Essai sur l'avenir poétique de Dieu. Bossuet, Pascal, Chateaubriand, Claudel* (Paris: Plon, 1965), p. 230.

17. "Les plus grands penseurs, depuis Aristote, se sont attaqués à ce problème, qui toujours se dérobe sous l'effort, glisse, s'échappe, se redresse, impertinent défi jeté à la spéculation philosophique"—Bergson, *Oeuvres*, p. 387.

18. "Pascal belongs to that class of men who cannot be defined"—Guardini, p. 12.

touch more closely than those who grasp the evanescent
quality of his style. Mr. Wells notes: "All of Pascal's
thought has an existential quality. His ideas are lumi-
nous sparks, struck by the encounter of person with
reality, of intellect with event. 'The style is the
man'. . . . "[19] Mr. Alcorn sees all Pascal's images as
characterized by an "extraordinary flatness, a lack of
third dimension" (p. 24), as "a series of unconnected but
sharp visual images" (p. 31). Does this not suggest the
fractured technique of modern abstract painting? And
does not modern painting carry its heavy burden of
awkwardness, and discord, and horror? In Mr. Chestov's
words: "Pascal's *Pensées* are only a description of the
abyss."[20]

Pascal proceeds rapidly from one level to another
of a problem, using all the destructive tones of ridicule
as a springboard, and he is consistent in his techniques.
He opens a question of morals by forestalling the argument of the libertine: "Ceux qui sont dans le dérèglement
disent à ceux qui sont dans l'ordre que ce sont eux qui
s'éloignent de la nature, et ils la croient suivre . . . "
(697). The freethinker may then in common sense consider his point of view as possibly ridiculous and illogical, through the trick of a visual image common to the
experience of us all: "comme ceux qui sont dans un vaisseau croient que ceux qui sont au bord fuient." Having
attacked, Pascal admits, disarmingly, ruefully, the
weakness of rhetoric as such, his own as well as that
of his adversary: "Le langage est pareil de tous côtés."
Ridicule here means a glimpse of the deceptive resemblance of opposites. He must then trick himself and the

19. Albert N. Wells, *Pascal's Recovery of Man's Wholeness* (Richmond, Va.: John Knox, 1965), p. 18.
20. Leo Chestov, *In Job's Balances. On the Sources of the Eternal
Truths* (London: J. M. Dent & Sons, 1932), p. 311.

reader with practical logic: "Il faut un point fixe pour en juger. Le port juge ceux qui sont dans un vaisseau, . . . " (Montalte has not disappeared from the scene). The reader, however, will have admitted the generality of "un point fixe" at his peril. Pascal's final question, " . . . mais où prendrons-nous un port dans la morale?", wrenches a thinker out of the framework of accepted moral codes and throws him into the uncertain realms of relativity in morals.

If the constant break-up of institutions and traditions represents the abyss that eternally faces us,[21] part of Pascal's answer in the *Pensées* is the value of the objectivity of humor for persuasion, for self-analysis, and for possible solution, always on a new level.

It is precisely on a new, and old, level that Pascal seeks his "point fixe", for he will not remain, with Molière and La Fontaine, on a secular plane. He has no hesitation in challenging the whole structure of rationality which has been a crowning glory of Western civilization.

Pascal uses humor persistently to break through crystallized patterns of thought, to shatter the barriers of smugly accepted truths, however vast their implications, to keep us thoroughly dissatisfied with our conceptions and indeed with many of the greatest ideas presented to us in our culture. Humor is for him above all dynamic and aimed at the discovery of the always more ultimate truth which inevitably and constantly escapes us. In that respect, humor is eminently constructive. The process is the proof of the dignity of

21. " . . . Nous voguons sur un milieu vaste, toujours incertains et flottants, poussés d'un bout vers l'autre; quelque terme où nous pensions nous attacher et nous affermir, il branle et nous quitte, et si nous le suivons, il échappe à nos prises, nous glisse et nous fuit d'une fuite éternelle; rien ne s'ârrete pour nous. C'est l'état qui nous est naturelle . . . tout notre fondement craque et la terre s'ouvre jusqu'aux abîmes" (199).

man. The courage to prick all balloons of vanity, even all pride in knowledge, is evidence of the deepest idealism and optimism. "Jamais [il] ne négocie. Sans cesse il provoque. Il voit autrement, il nous veut différents."[22] This balancing effect of the destruction of illusion Pascal shows in the poetic arrangement of one of the *Pensées*, evident in the manuscript:

> S'il se vante, je l'abaisse
> S'il s'abaisse, je le vante
> Et le contredis toujours
> jusqu'à ce qu'il comprenne
> qu'il est un monstre incompréhensible. (130)[23]

There is no way then to get through to truth but to portray illusion, exhibit contradiction, render them clearly ridiculous. Without such destruction and death of ideas no rebirth on a higher level is possible.

His humor makes man smile, always at himself, and inexorably Pascal's sincerity drives his point home, for he never fails in the social grace or the profound humility which applies his every ridicule to himself. With what delicacy he suggests Baudelaire's tragic "mon semblable, mon frère". He takes the personal bitterness of a La Rochefoucauld out of the subject of *l'amour-propre*, but his attack on self-love is no less profound. Vanity obviously invades even his desire to

22. André Dodin, "Préface" to *Pensées*, ed. Lafuma (Paris: Seuil, 1962), p. 7.

23. *Le manuscrit des Pénsees de Pascal, 1662.* Lafuma ed. (Paris: Les Libraires Associés, 1962), 130:

> S'il se vante—je l abaisse
> S'il s abesse, je le vante
> Et le contredis toujour
> jusqu a se qu'il comprainne
> qu'il est÷ng monstre÷conpreansible.

Further references to the manuscript will be to this edition.

communicate through his work the most telling message of his life and the artistic form he wishes it to take: "La vanité est si ancrée dans le coeur de l'homme qu'un soldat, un goujat, un cuisinier, un crocheteur se vante et veut avoir ses admirateurs et les philosophes mêmes en veulent, et ceux qui écrivent contre veulent avoir la gloire d'avoir bien écrit, et ceux qui les lisent veulent avoir la gloire de les avoir lus, et moi qui écris ceci ai peut-être cette envie, et peut-être que ceux qui le liront . . . " (627). It is Pascal who leaves the sentence unfinished, gently and gracefully laughing at his reader, as at himself. This engaging approach to accomplish the fall of the proud, to abase *le moi* "haïssable" is gentle, telling humor, the true language of the *honnête homme*.

The conclusion he wishes to reach through humor is not gentle but profound. Even as he declares *le moi* "haïssable par sa concupiscence" (564), he renders even self-love constructive, redeems it by raising it to a spiritual level, for the universal good is in us. "Le royaume de Dieu est en nous. Le bien universel . . . est nous-même et n'est pas nous" (564).

Themes: The Application of Humor. Reason, Love, Death, Chance

Pascal applies the weapon of humor to the most important areas in life, to the insufficiency of reason (attacking where one is proudest), to love, death, chance, war, government, justice, the beauty and efficacy of art, the pursuit of happiness, and to practical life, the busyness of the modern person, charlatanry in medicine, general direction in education, the choice of a trade, even order in writing a book. All of these considerations turn endlessly around the basic questions of human existence to which he refers so often, in language that changes as little as the diversity in his portrayal of illusion is great: " . . . l'homme sans lumière . . . comme égaré dans ce recoin de l'univers sans savoir qui l'y a mis, ce qu'il y est venu faire, ce qu'il deviendra en mourant" (198), or again: "Qu'ont-ils trouvé [les philosophes] de son origine, de sa durée et de son départ?" (76), or "l'ordre de la pensée est de commencer par soi, et par son auteur et sa fin" (620).

Themes: reason.

With an arched eyebrow and a quirk of the lips, he considers the limits of reason, the attitude of Descartes, and the whole of modern scientific method and faith. M. Chevalier refers to Menjot's comment in 1697: "Feu M.

Pascal appelait la philosophie cartésienne le roman de
la nature, semblable à peu près à l'histoire de Don
Qhichot."[1] Clear satire, even by the comparison. As man
is only "un roseau, le plus faible de la nature" (200),
capable of being destroyed by inanimate force and
dignified only by reason, so this same weakness is transposed to the intellectual plane: "Faiblesse. . . . Il en
est de même de la science. Car la maladie l'ôte" (28).
M. Steinmann has noted that Pascal's attitude toward
science does not lack humor: "répugnance de la nature
pour le vide . . . Cette répugnance n'est pas plus 'grande
pour admettre un grand vide qu'un petit'."[2] The scientist
suffers from this deftly belittling humor, though nature,
personified, takes the blame on the surface.

What is the result of faith in reason from Montaigne
on, but skepticism and relativism? " . . . notre raison
est toujours déçue par l'inconstance des apparences . . . " (199). This is the humiliating joke played
on humans: "Voilà où nous mènent les connaissances
naturelles. Si celles-là ne sont véritables il n'y a point
de vérité dans l'homme, et si elles le sont il y trouve un
grand sujet d'humiliation, forcé de s'abaisser d'une ou
d'autre manière" (199). Pascal states directly: "Rien
suivant la seule raison n'est juste de soi, tout branle
avec le temps" (60). Yet he is just as capable of reaching
a conclusion on the multiplicity of human errors with
light irony, implicit in the adverb, "heureusement", or
the adjective, "excellents", incongruously linked to
"le faux": "L'homme est donc si heureusement fabriqué
qu'il n'a aucun principe juste du vrai, et plusieurs
excellents du faux" (44).[3] Irony through an adjective
occurs frequently: "*Plaisante* raison qu'un vent manie et

1. *Oeuvres*, Pléiade ed., p. 1504. Note to p. 1137.
2. Jean Steinmann, *Pascal* (Bruges, Belgium: Desclée De Brouwer,
1962), p. 48.
3. The irony appreciated, but expressed slightly less concisely,

à tous sens. . . . Jamais la raison (ne surmonte) totalement l'imagination, (mais le) contraire est ordinaire" (44). One sees "Plaisante justice" (60). Pascal is equally apt with direct and heavy sarcasm: " . . . De la confusion de Montaigne . . . de dire des sottises par hasard et par faiblesse c'est un mal ordinaire, mais d'en dire par dessein c'est ce qui n'est pas supportable . . ." (780).

More directly amusing and vivid is the image of the philosopher on a plank over a precipice: "Le plus grand philosophe du monde sur une planche plus large qu'il ne faut, s'il y a au-dessous un précipice, quoique sa raison le convainque de sa sûreté, son imagination prévaudra. Plusieurs n'en sauraient soutenir la pensée sans pâlir et suer" (44). The choice of the philosopher in the picture is humorous hyperbole and in no way diminishes application of the example to all humans.

It is by a haunting image, also a universal one, that Pascal disarms the reader in ridiculing reliance upon reason: " . . . personne n'a d'assurance, hors de la foi —s'il veille ou s'il dort, vu que durant le sommeil on croit veiller aussi fermement que nous faisons. . . . On croit voir les espaces, les figures, les mouvements, on sent couler le temps, on le mesure, et enfin on agit de même qu'éveillé. De sorte que la moitié de la vie se passant en sommeil, par notre propre aveu ou quoiqu'il nous en paraisse, nous n'avons aucune idée du vrai, tous nos sentiments étant alors des illusions" (131).

---

by Fontenelle in *Histoire des oracles* (1687), 1ère Dissertation, Chap. IV: "Cela veut dire que non seulement nous n'avons pas les principes qui mènent au vrai, mais que nous en avons d'autres qui s'accommodent très-bien avec le faux." It is much in the spirit and tone of Fontenelle's dry remark two paragraphs earlier: "Assurons-nous bien du fait, avant que de nous inquiéter de la cause . . . nous éviterons le ridicule d'avoir trouvé la cause de ce qui n'est point"—Bernard Le Bovier de Fontenelle, *Oeuvres complètes* (Genève: Slatkine Reprints, 1968), 3 vol. Réimpression de l'édition de Paris, 1818.

The image has an evanescent quality, the delicacy of dreams or smoke, heightened by the poetic use of v's and f's, s's and liquids. It is insidious in its gentle capacity for creating a powerful effect, almost a soporific, so that one is caught up short with the cutting and intransigent conclusion: "nous n'avons aucune idée du vrai." The comedy is in the sudden reversal of style, the almost imperceptible transition to the final blow, the grand frustration.

There is also another quality, notable in his images in general. All is movement: on voit "les *mouvements*, on sent *couler* le temps, on le *mesure*, . . . on *agit*" (as in all of Molière one sees oneself in action on the stage). So inherent and necessary is this mobile, dramatic quality of the image for Pascal's thought that this movement cannot stop, the image transposes itself by its own impetus to the next plane. Indeed, the negative conclusion, on the way, only serves this purpose. "Qui sait si cette autre moitié de la vie où nous pensons veiller n'est pas un autre sommeil un peu différent du premier . . . dont nous nous éveillons quand nous pensons dormir . . . " (131). This new suggestion, this new destruction and death of the possibility of reality in waking life—is this the conclusion? No, the image is still in movement and has still the evanescent quality of a smoke screen. It can clear at any moment for the higher vision suggested, for the rebirth to higher reality, for the more real and living existence. One does not say "most", for where is the ultimate in spiritual movement? When does one stop? Is not this movement of continual elevation its most essential quality? The image Pascal chose is drama already assimilated to the spiritual level of thought. It is an arrow, a projectile, shot into the spaces of the spiritual universe. The constant impetus is the temporary frustration of self-deception. For the movement of the soul to take place, man must stand outside of himself so that his faulty perception becomes ludicrous.

The courage of this approach through the comic vision is Pascal's natural way of thinking. He could not dwell in the skepticism of a Montaigne, he could not luxuriate in the despair of many existentialists, though he has felt it as deeply: "En voyant . . . l'homme . . . incapable de toute connaissance, j'entre en effroi, comme un homme qu'on aurait porté endormi dans une île déserte et effroyable, et qui s'éveillerait sans connaître où il est, et sans moyen d'en sortir. Et sur cela, j'admire comment on n'entre point en désespoir d'un si misérable état" (198). His tragic symbol, presented in the first person, serves only as a prelude, and the entering into despair is stated as a negative and as subordinate to a wondering. The verb, *j'admire*, has its satirical effect, pointing up illusion again, as if he wished for a real despair in everyone (the pronoun has changed to the impersonal *on*) through clarity of vision that would lead to new thought and action.

So he speaks to the modern person, foreseeing, perhaps, in the specific movement of his time (and in the timeless pride of humans) the era when science would become a god. His satirical expression is more persuasive than many modern echoes of his thoughts, such as: " . . . La froide intelligence fait cela quelquefois, elle devient comme une idole qui barre la route du Paradis. L'homme le plus intelligent ne l'est pas toujours assez pour comprendre que cette intelligence doit être dépassée et non adorée pour elle-même."[4] Einstein, ushering in the age of relativity, expresses it thus: "Ignoring the realities of faith, goodwill, and honesty in seeking a solu-

4. Julien Green, *Vers l'invisible (1958-1967)* (Paris: Plon, 1967), p. 87.

tion, we place too much faith in legalisms, treaties, and mechanisms. . . . Science has brought forth this danger, but the real problem is in the minds and hearts of men."[5] Pascal, with succinct irony, goes to the heart of the matter: "C'est une chose déplorable de voir tous les hommes ne délibérer que des moyens et point de la fin" (193).

Themes: love.

In its search for universality, the French theater of the seventeenth century did confine itself to the minds and hearts of human beings. Tragedy, gradually through Corneille to Racine, concentrated on that most universal theme of love. Though Molière's comedy ranges more widely, the situation of love and, by extension, family remain the pivot or, as it were, the prism through which other themes sift, clarify, and illuminate their various facets. The approach of comedy claims the freer treatment and the wider horizons.

For Pascal the theme of love is no less central, nor does he neglect its principal aspects. He gives it its greatest horizons and a cosmic setting for *le coeur*. The theme of love in the classic theater is always essentially of the mind and of the heart, *l'amour passion* and *l'amour estime* and, for Molière, retains its aspects of inexplicable charm, good sense, and the force of nature.

Unless one accepts Pascal's authorship of the *Discours sur les passions de l'amour*,[6] his treatment of *l'amour passion* in the *Pensées* is brief enough but not lacking in

5. Albert Einstein, "Only Then Shall We Find Courage." Reprinted from the *New York Times Magazine*. Pamphlet issued by the Emergency Committee of Atomic Scientists (May 21, 1947), p. 3.

6. which seems possible to M. Chevalier and others (see M. Baudouin's discussion, pp. 59-60), but not to M. Lafuma (Pascal, *Oeuvres*, p. 285). M. Lafuma confirms his opinion in his *Histoire des Pensées de Pascal (1656-1952)* (Paris: Nizet, 1969), pp. 107, 112.

depth and appears certainly in comic perspective. Nothing could be more condensed or effective than the image of Cleopatra's nose (413). M. Jerphagnon has been impressed by the element of incongruousness: "l'amour fait plutôt figure de catastrophe que d'événement heureux."[7] This whole conception of earthly love becomes an illusion: "Qui voudra connaître à plein la vanité de l'homme . . . " (413) and "Vanité. La cause et les effets de l'amour. Cléopâtre" (46), a *figure*, a prefiguration of the love of God.

What does he see in the distortion of the illusion which is, in comedy, the mask through which one must read truth? What are the *étranges disproportions*? The inexplicable charm of *l'amour-passion* (Corneille's "un je ne sais quoi") is accorded its full importance as pivot, the force that moves princes, armies, the whole earth. The disporportion between the apparent insignificance of the cause and the disaster that can follow in it wake ("les effets en sont effroyables") has all the mystery and again the charming illusiveness (witness the choice of the famous example of feminine beauty) of the element of chance (*le hasard*, which will so fascinate Voltaire throughout his novels) and its results in the chain of cause and effect through history. This is the "dynamique de l'absurde" which is for M. Demorest the "reflet d'une ironie divine", the déséquilibre savant", the "clef lointaine", the "secret" of Pascal's thought.[8]

This does not diminish the danger of *l'amour-passion*, felt so strongly in classical tragedy (in *Andromaque*, in *Phèdre*), or the disporportion inherent in the attraction of opposites (Alceste and Célimène).

7. Lucien Jerphagnon, *Le Caractère de Pascal. Essai de caractérologie littéraire* (Paris: Presses Universitaires de France, 1962), p. 247.

8. Jean-Jacques Demorest, "Pascal et le déséquilibre," *PMLA* (May, 1967), pp. 194 & 196.

Let us note that the interesting passage on love and
the dangers of comedy (*Pensées*, 764) is apparently not
Pascal's. M. Lafuma indicates that it was published in
the *Maximes* of l'abbé d'Ailly in 1678 and accepts it as
being written by Mme de Sablé.[9] Found among Pascal's
papers, it was included in the copy of the *Pensées* (B.N.
9203). It is impossible to check handwriting; in the
facsimile edition of the original manuscript, the number
"764" carries the notation: "original perdu".

Yet Pascal kept it among his papers. Is this testimony
to his awareness of the danger inherent in the charm
and beauty of art which can take on its own intangible
quality of illusion? One thinks inevitably of Racine's
withdrawal from the theater after *Phèdre*, of Tolstoy's
Kreutzer Sonata.[10] Pascal is apparently interested in
the idea of the insidious attractiveness of comedy, its
detached delicacy and lightness of illusion: "Tous les
grands divertissements sont dangereux pour la vie
chrétienne; . . . il n'y en à point qui soit plus à craindre
que la comédie" (764). However, he continues to use
the persuasive value of laughter. Does his persistence
make the fear of the artistic portrayal of love in comic
perspective also an illusion and the love of God evidence
of truth?[11] Had not Corneille's concept already evolved
through the intellectual value of *l'amour-estime* to the
purified passion of Polyeucte?

The deep fear of classicism is always for uncontrolled

9. Pascal, *Oeuvres complètes*, l'Intégrale (Seuil, 1963), p. 666:
"En fait, pour de multiples raisons, comme le pensait Victor Cousin,
il est bien de la marquise."

10. M. Baudouin has the same thought: " . . . jugements sur les
arts . . . que l'on songe à Racine, à Tolstoi" (p. 38). But M. Baudouin,
strangely, like M. Guardini, seems to exclude any appreciation of art
on Pascal's part, except a severely intellectual perspective.

11. "Tu ne me chercherais pas, si tu ne me possédais. Ne t'inquiète
donc pas" (929).

love. Thus, the image of *l'éternuement*, much commented upon, stresses the involuntary aspect in love, as well as the distortion in the will that allows itself to be satisfied with illusion: "Or il n'y a que la maîtrise et l'empire qui fasse la gloire, et que la servitude qui fasse honte" (795). Pascal finds the human dilemma to be this inherent division between passion and reason: "Guerre intestine de l'homme entre la raison et les passions. . . . Aussi il est toujours divisé et contraire à lui-même" (621).

The effect of flux, of relativity in the area of love lends itself to comic treatment. What is the human position but one of frustration and helplessness? Love does not go in a straight line; unexpectedly, it is all changed. After ten years the lover stands dismayed, bewildered, non-plussed, resigned (?), like Candide (in spite of all his goodwill and devotion) before the ravaged Cunégonde: "Il n'aime plus cette personne qu'il aimait il y a dix ans. Je crois bien: elle n'est plus la même ni lui non plus. Il était jeune et elle aussi; elle est tout autre. Il l'aimerait peut-être encore telle qu'elle était alors" (673). This bewilderment can extend to the institution of marriage. Pascal does not protect the concept of marriage as Molière does. His point of view is more detached. Mar-riage, being a human institution, remains a compromise: " . . . que dira [-t-] on qui soit bon? La chasteté? Je dis que non, car le monde finirait. Le mariage? non, la continence vaut mieux" (905). For Pascal, even marriage enters into the realm of the absurd. This is the human dilemma: " . . . Nous n'avons ni vrai ni bien qu'en partie, et mêlé de mal et de faux" (905).

The impression of evanescence is applied more widely, and with the incessant repetition of the verb *aimer*, to the very modern question of self-identification. The application of reason renders the possibility absurd.

Qu'est-ce que le moi?

. . . celui qui aime quelqu'un à cause de sa beauté, l'aime-t-il? Non: car la petite vérole, qui tuera la beauté sans tuer la personne, fera qu'il ne l'aimera plus.

Et si on m'aime pour mon jugement, pour ma mémoire, m'aime-t-on? *moi*? Non, car je puis perdre ces qualités sans me perdre moi-même. Où est donc ce *moi*, s'il n'est ni dans le corps, ni dans l'âme? et comment aimer le corps ou l'âme, sinon pour ces qualités, qui ne sont point ce qui fait le moi, puisqu'elles sont périssables? car aimerait-on la substance de l'âme d'une personne, abstraitement, et quelques qualités qui y fussent? Cela ne se peut, et serait injuste. On n'aime donc jamais personne, mais seulement des qualités.

. . . on n'aime personne que pour des qualités empruntées (688).

Thus the cause of love—"la cause et les effets de l'amour. Cléopâtre" (46), classed as "Vanité"—remains eminently mysterious and the effects frightful to behold.

If one borders on serious language to paint the absurdity of illusion, it is to be remembered that Philinthe speaks as seriously in *le Misanthrope*. It is the absurdity of the situation under consideration that makes it comedy, comedy exerting itself to tear away the veil of illusion, to carry us higher to the element of truth.

The modern psychologist says the vision must be other than it is for people. One must love and respect the self or one will be incapable of loving others. For Pascal, vision through contradictions is dynamic: "Contrariétés. . . . la bassesse et la grandeur de l'homme. Que l'homme maintenant s'estime son prix. . . . Qu'il se haïsse, qu'il s'aime: il a en lui la capacité de connaître la vérité et d'être heureux; mais il n'a point de vérité, ou constante, ou satisfaisante" (119).

The dilemma now exists on a new plane, and we are still in movement: "Tous les corps ensemble et tous les esprits ensemble, et toutes leurs productions ne valent pas le moindre mouvement de charité." Charity is a movement. "De tous les corps et esprits, on n'en saurait tirer un mouvement de vraie charité, cela est impossible, d'un autre ordre surnaturel" (308). We are in the timeless concept of the thirteenth chapter of I Corinthians. We are, in the recent terms of Erich Fromm's *Art of Loving*,[12] to get away from narcissism to a true concept of what love is. This illusion of narcissism, too, Pascal indicates with humor: "Notre propre intérêt est encore un merveilleux instrument pour nous crever les yeux agréablement" (44). Irony results from the sequence of the adjective "merveilleux" (one extreme), the verb "crever" (the opposite extreme, the surprise), and the second surprise, reversal, when one thought the juxtaposition of extremes was accomplished, in the adverb "agréablement".

We are beyond the intellectual level, which carries its own burden of illusion: "On se fait idole de la vérité même, car le vérité hors de la charité n'est pas Dieu, et est son image et une idole qu'il ne faut point aimer ni adorer, et encore moins faut-il aimer ou adorer son contraire, qui est le mensonge" (926). We are in the true domain of *le coeur* and still in movement. We are involved as the existentialist requires; and the sole positive principle he seems to have been able to enunciate is in effect the movement of charity: solidarity, fraternity, involvement for one's fellow human.

Pascal carries one into the highest and most difficult

12. This work contains most interesting passages on levels of conversation and on silence and techniques of meditation. Cf. Pascal: ". . . l'homme fait lui seul une conversation intérieure, qu'il importe de bien régler. . . . Il faut se tenir en silence autant qu'on peut, et ne s'entretenir que de Dieu, qu'on sait être la vérité; et ainsi on se la persuade à soi-même" (99).

freedom and with it to joy: one's involvement must find
its form of manifestation before the tribunal of God.
There can be no greater dignity attributed to self. The
resultant joy is in the process, but joy is the other side
of suffering. He affirms that "je ne puis approuver que
ceux qui cherchent en gémissant" (405). What he has
found and constantly seeks again is the God of *Mémorial*: "le Dieu d'Abraham, le Dieu d'Isaac, le Dieu de
Jacob, le Dieu des chrétiens, est un Dieu d'amour et de
consolation . . . , de joie . . . " (449). This is the joy in
growth which Baudelaire sees in a child's laughter.

Are the other forms of humor a prevision and a
promise of this joy of a lost Eden and of salvation?

Themes: death

Death is a cardinal fact. Here one comes upon the
kind of gigantic, sad, or bitter humor to be found in
Shakespeare's *Hamlet*, or reflected in the skepticism
of Montaigne, or as the foundation of the existentialist's
concept of the absurd, which is projected to a cosmic
level by this inescapable first condition. It is so important, so unavoidable, and so humiliating a fact that a
first reaction for the human being in his pride is not to
think of it, and this becomes a prime motive for diversion, for incessant distraction, indeed for the will to
seek and perpetrate illusion in order to make the suffering as momentary as possible: "Divertissement. La
mort est plus aisée à supporter sans y penser que la
pensée de mort sans péril" (138). The avoidance implies
recognition that the fact of death is almost too great and
too dangerous to handle. Pascal's sentence is a juxtaposition of words that makes one think one can still smile at
the aptness of language and postpone the peril of thinking. Author joins reader in playing at self-deception.

However, the challenge is laid down clearly. How

shall one respond to it? Obviously, not by avoidance for Pascal. He has little respect for the answer in Montaigne's skepticism, as representing another kind of evasion. It is an ironic dismissal of whatever effort is implied in the word *essai* to declare that "il ne pense qu'à mourir lâchement et mollement par tout son livre" (680).

Courage is the note, to face the fact fully, to admit it, to absorb it. Pascal is a realist.

We emerge from illusion and comedy to face a truth: "Le dernier acte est sanglant, quelque belle que soit la comédie en tout le reste. On jette enfin de la terre sur la tête et en voilà pour jamais" (165). It is to be noted that this *pensée* is placed in the *liasse* entitled *Commencement*. In an unclassified *pensée*, the whole inescapable thought is set into its larger setting, and by the concept of the word "éternel", a new door opens, for "il est indubitable que le temps de cette vie n'est qu'un instant, que l'état de la mort est éternel, de quelque nature qu'il puisse être . . . " (428). In the last phrase new doubt and new hope come into being. In this perspective of the infinite, the perpetual axis of his thought, Pascal views the dilemma and the absurdity, the comedy, of the human position. He ridicules his utter ignorance: the only thing he knows for sure is that about which he knows nothing. The total mystery is in the context of immortality. "Tout ce que je connais est que je dois bientôt mourir; mais ce que j'ignore le plus est cette mort même que je ne saurais éviter. Comme je ne sais d'où je viens, aussi je ne sais où je vais . . . " (427). Death is a central mystery.

On this plane, also, imagery, comedy and ridicule operate intertwined. A dramatic scene flashes on. With the detachment of comic perspective one is forced to look upon oneself acting out one's despair: "Qu'on s'imagine un nombre d'hommes dans les chaînes, et tous

condamnés à la mort, dont les uns étant chaque jour
égorgés à la vue des autres, ceux qui restent voient leur
propre condition dans celle de leurs semblables, et, se
regardant les uns les autres avec douleur et sans
espérance, attendent à leur tour. C'est l'image de la
condition des hommes" (434). Is this clear tragedy?
No, ridicule is underlined and implied. This image is
different from those we have already noted. It stands
out by its static quality. The one active word is "égorgés",
and that verb is in the passive; man is acted upon. The
others are static: "restent", "se regardant", "attendent".
This is humiliation. This is a human being in chains,
knowing the conditions, seeing and passively accepting
this state, a slave with no impulse to freedom in his
soul. Pascal attacks the static stance, ridiculing despair.

What impulse should one have? This static being is
not a whole person. A man seeks, a man acts, even if
he ventures out in error: "Tous les hommes recherchent
d'être heureux. . . . Ce qui fait que les uns vont à la
guerre et que les autres n'y vont pas est ce même désir
qui est dans tous les deux accompagné de différentes
vues. . . . C'est le motif de toutes les actions de tous
les hommes, jusqu'à ceux qui vont se pendre" (148).
The surprise ending provokes the smile, points up the
ridicule. Yet the stimulus is powerful. Even the suicide
has courage; he does not stand and wait; he acts, even
if negatively. Error, contradictions, illusions are implicit in the pursuit of happiness, in risks of death and
possibilities of life.

When death is placed in its setting of the infinite,
imagery plays its usual role, providing the veil that
hides and reveals truth, that opens the door to the possibility of immortality, and wins our hearts and minds
by a marriage of art and logic: "la moitié de notre vie
se passant en sommeil, par notre propre aveu. . . . Qui

sait si cette autre moitié de la vie où nous pensons veiller
n'est pas un autre sommeil un peu différent du premier
. . . dont nous nous éveillons quand nous pensons
dormir . . . " (131).[13] This dynamic doubt, this possibility, this vision becomes a justification for the act
of faith. The artistic use of illusion and self-deception
with its accompanying irony is likewise dynamic, positive, essentially constructive. It is from the vivid con-
densation of a metaphor within a metaphor that thought
springs up, as if concentric circles could express the
unity of existence and transform successive doubts into
creative thought and the very movement of life.

Themes: chance.

The cosmic vision expresses itself in metaphor upon
metaphor for this joke on humanity, a bubble of illusion
to be broken in the effort to discover truth. Reason
observes inescapably the element of chance in human
destiny. Chance will take a predominant place in the
intellectual bias of Voltaire, expressed in comedy, in
irony. What does chance become in Pascal's thought?
It is disproportion, heightened by its movement in the
chain of historical cause and effect, that is, the effects
of passion on history, linked with a small physical fact
over which there was no control, *le nez de Cléopâtre*
(413). This is not a one-time impression for Pascal. He
speaks more than once of the effects of illness on what
one might expect as a reasonable course. Illness takes
its place among the elements of chance in the great
events of history: "Cromwell allait ravager toute la
chrétienté; la famille royale était perdue, et la sienne à
jamais puissante sans un petit grain de sable qui se mit
dans son uretère. Rome même allait trembler sous lui.
Mais ce gravier s'étant mis là, il est mort, sa famille

13. "la vie est un songe un peu moins inconstant" (803).

abaissée, tout en paix, et le roi rétabli" (750). The
concrete cause is even smaller here; and there is no
passion, no beauty involved. Man's humiliation is therefore deeper and thrown into relief by the vastness of
his pretentions: the thwarted attack against "la chrétienté". The antithesis of the small and the vast, the ugly
and the beautiful, moves in history, in the spiritual realm
and in the physical: "La puissance des mouches, elles
gagnent des batailles, empêchent notre âme d'agir,
mangent notre corps" (22). The swarming of the insects,
the movement of the image, overpowers one. The small
cause and the vast result form striking antithesis to
point up the mocking mystery of the universe.

A group of *pensées* goes very interestingly together
(these variously included in the unclassified papers,
Series XXIII, XXIV, & XXV). Pascal crossed out a wry
observation on memory: "Hasard donne les pensées, et
hasard les ôte. Point d'art pour conserver ni pour ac-
quérir" (542). In this, the mind is at the mercy of chance.
In different and positive form he retained it: "La mémoire
est nécessaire pour toutes les opérations de la raison"
(651). He suppressed, likewise, an ironic thought on the
power of the subconscious, on unconscious self-
deception: "Pensée échappée, je la voulais écrire;
j'écris au lieu, qu'elle m'est échappée" (542). One is
helpless to control his reason or his fate? He retained
it in positive form: "En écrivant ma pensée elle m'échappe
quelquefois; mais cela me fait souvenir de ma faiblesse
que j'oublie à toute heure, ce qui m'instruit autant que
ma pensée oubliée, car je ne tiens qu'à connaître mon
néant" (656). The seed of greatness is there, uncovered
by the effectiveness of irony: weakness can be contem-
plated, known, used. In the sentence, chance has taken the
smaller place, as the first in a chain of three movements.

Chance becomes the cloak of other forces in important

and extremely practical areas. Custom becomes an element of chance. The ridicule is again inherent in antithesis: "La chose la plus importante à toute la vie est le choix du métier, le hasard en dispose. La coutume fait les maçons, soldats, couvreurs" (634). The comedy plays itself out; we hear the actors: "C'est un excellent couvreur, dit-on; et en parlant des soldats: ils sont bien fous, dit-on, et les autres au contraire: il n'y a rien de grand que la guerre, le reste des hommes sont des coquins." The derogatory terms of ordinary speech, "fous" and "coquins", make the speakers come alive. The contrast with condescending epithets ("excellents", "grand") provokes the laugh. There is a suggestion that custom is not entirely blind: "on choisit. Car naturellement on aime la vertu et on hait la folie; ces mots mêmes décideront; on ne pèche qu'en l'application." The circles of absurd effect widen: "de ceux que la nature n'a fait qu'hommes, on fait toutes les conditions des hommes. Car des pays sont tout de maçons, d'autres tout de soldats, etc., . . . c'est la coutume qui fait donc cela, car elle contraint la nature, et quelquefois la nature la surmonte, et retient l'homme dans son instinct malgré toute coutume bonne ou mauvaise." Two levels of langage operate here, the concrete, "maçons", "soldats", and the convolutions of abstract thought. The welding of the two give artistic body to the sense of movement, of growth that is the mark of life. The seed of greatness is not to be held down. Man moves. Even with the consideration of custom we have touched upon a new level with its own new questions. "La nature recommence toujours . . . ainsi se fait une espèce d'infini et d'etérnel" (663).

When the thought about choice of occupation is carried over to the section (XV) classified as "Transition", it is set clearly into the perspective of the infinite: "C'est une chose déplorable de voir tous les hommes ne délibérer que des moyens et point de la fin . . . pour le choix de la condition . . . le sort nous le donne . . . c'est ce qui détermine chacun à chaque condition de serrurier, soldat, etc." (193).

Chance also takes the name of justice, the masquerade provoking much ridicule. The diversity of human laws with the influences such as custom and climate that produce them, which will so take hold of the mind of Montesquieu, is not new to Pascal's thought, but it presents itself differently. Pascal is not concerned less with the spirit of laws and basic principles, but the contradictions become a vast comedy: "Sur quoi fondera [-t-] il l'économie du monde qu'il veut gouverner? Sera-ce sur le caprice de chaque particulier? Quelle confusion! sera-ce sur la justice? il l'ignore" (60). As for universal principles, how is one to take them seriously? "Certainement, s'il la connaissait il n'aurait pas établi cette maxime, la plus générale de toutes celles qui sont parmi les hommes, que chacun suive les moeurs de sons pays . . . les législateurs n'auraient pas pris pour modèle . . . les fantasies et les caprices des perses et allemands. . . . on ne voit rien de juste ou d'injuste qui ne change de qualité en changeant de climat, trois degrés d'élévation du pôle renversent toute la jurisprudence, un méridien décide de la vérité . . . le droit a ses époques. . . . " The tone is unmistakable: "Plaisante justice qu'une rivière borne. Vérité au-deça des Pyrénées, erreur au-delà." Words offered as synonyms in the sentence, patently opposite in meaning, create the impression of absurdity: "prendre pour *modèle* les *fantaisies* et les *caprices*". Mathematical exactness is used to undermine abstract rules; from two levels superimposed spring the impression of absurdity and new thought: "*un méridien* décide de *la vérité*" and "*justice* qu'*une rivière* borne". "La

vérité" displaced into physical space becomes "erreur".
Close juxtaposition of opposite words on one level or of
two very different levels superimposed give form to the
paradox of existence.

Man claims that "la justice . . . réside dans les lois
naturelles communes en tout pays" (60) and would
maintain it: "si la témérité du hasard qui a semé les lois
humaines en avait rencontré au moins une qui fût uni-
verselle. Mais la plaisanterie est telle que le caprice des
hommes s'est si bien diversifié qu'il n'y en a point." The
sentence piles up comic effects and tones: the calm
condescension of the general rule; the personification
of chance, "la témérité du hasard", in which chance
becomes inimical; the sweeping casual gesture of sowing
seed, "a semé", as against the positive sound of "les lois",
the concept of an absolute; the casualness of "avait
rencontré" (met by chance) as over against "au moins
une" to ridicule the possibility of universal laws. Justice
is laughable when pinned down to concrete fact and
common sense.

If the strongest examples are needed to destroy the
illusion, sarcasm and invective effectively replace irony:
"Le larcin, l'inceste, le meurtre des enfants et des pères,
tout a eu sa place entre les actions vertueuses" (60). The
antithesis of the concrete crime and the abstract idea of
virtue throws grotesque shadows upon the screen of
truth. "Se peut-il rien de plus plaisant, qu'un homme
ait droit de me tuer parcequ'il demeure au-delà de l'eau
et que son prince a querelle contre le mien, quoique je
n'en ai aucune avec lui" (60).

Chance and justice are inextricably intertwined with
questions of government for proof of absurdity. Pascal
does not consider, like Montesquieu, the three basic
forms of government but takes his example from the
form before him. Monarchy is based on chance, on suc-

cession by birth. A mocking metaphor makes the concept absurd: "On ne choisit pas pour gouverner un vaisseau celui des voyageurs qui est de la meilleure maison"
(30 & 977).[14] Human vision is out of focus, but the law of
succession is practical. Pascal states a sure conviction,
the possibility of greater chaos: "Le plus grand des maux
est les guerres civiles. . . . Le mal à craindre d'un sot
qui succède par droit de naissance n'est ni si grand, ni si
sûr" (94). The ironic conclusion emerges: one stupid
choice is acceptable in order to avoid a greater folly.

The folly of violence, especially of civil war, illus-
trates the confusion that has placed justice "entre les
mains de la force. . . . De là vient l'injustice de la
Fronde, qui élève sa prétendue justice contre la force"
(85). This ironic invective in the word *prétendue* seems
directed against those who make civil war, yet it is kept
general, impersonal. Within his classification, *Raisons
des effets* (V, Classified papers), he indicates two levels:
"la force . . . une qualité palpable, . . . la justice . . .
une qualité spirituelle . . . " (85). From the shock of
this antithesis on a double level springs dynamic
thought: "Il n'en est pas de même dans l'Eglise, car il
y a une justice véritable et nulle violence" (85).

Security is illusion and the language supremely
ironic, with the irony condensed into the adverb "ad-
mirablement", after the bare suggestion of metaphor
or biblical parable in "pour fondement", a house built
upon sand: "La puissance des rois est fondée sur la
raison et sûr la folie du peuple, et bien plus sur la folie.
La plus grande et importante chose du monde a pour
fondement la faiblesse. Et ce fondement est admirable-
ment sûr . . . le peuple sera faible" (26). His recurrent
theme is ironic antithesis, the importance of issues and

14. Only this part of Nicole's passage (977) is in the handwriting
of Pascal (f° 83 of the ms., note of M. Chevalier, Pléiade, ed., p. 1505).

the weakness inherent in our choices. His invective is for man, universal man, in his misery and for the feebleness of reason: "Ce qui est fondé sur la saine raison est bien mal fondé, comme l'estime de la sagesse" (26).

His attack, bordering dangerously on the question of divine right, ridicules the people, deceived by appearances: "La coutume de voir les rois accompagnés de gardes, de tambours, . . . imprime dans leurs sujets le respect et la terreur . . . de là viennent ces mots: le caractère de la divinité est empreint sur son visage" (25).

Inevitably, Pascal meditates upon class structure in an aristocratic form of government, concluding that "tout le monde est dans l'illusion . . . [le] peuple . . . pense que la vérité est où elle n'est pas. . . . Il est vrai qu'il faut honorer les gentilshommes, mais non pas parce que la naissance est un avantage effectif" (92). He speaks through contradiction, "la vérité est où elle n'est pas", to imply the eternal theme of great satire that true nobility is very different from nobility of birth. The contradiction is between the practical choice and the perception which ought to exist. His antitheses force into one close image the practical or concrete and the spiritual or abstract. The double image (one superimposed on the other) is contained in the two meanings, specific and general, of the word "les gentilshommes".

The criticism is basic enough to rend the veil from existing illusion, to foresee the revolutionary generations of the eighteenth century. Was there also, as implicit in his thought as in Montesquieu's, the consideration of the march of democracy? When this thought emerges for him on the spiritual level, the term for the form of government is quite other than the practical seventeenth-century form of monarchy: "2 lois suffisent pour régler toute la République chrétienne, mieux que toutes les lois politiques" (376), so that the term "le royaume" is applicable only for "le royaume de Dieu". In the same section (Papiers classés, XXVI, Morale chrétienne) we find: "République. La République chrétienne et même judaïque n'a eu que Dieu pour maître comme remarque Philon Juif, *De la monarchie*. Quand ils combattaient ce n'était que pour Dieu et n'espéraient principalement que de Dieu" (369). We cannot help but note, too, the recurrence of the theme, "Opinions du peuple saines" (94, 95) and "Le peuple a les opinions très saines" (101). The caprice of human justice has bordered inexorably on the question of war.

The language of Pascal, with the control and force of classical impersonality, expresses itself in the terms of comic vision. If this presentation, or process, is to destroy an illusion, what is the illusion, and what direction is indicated?

In another *pensée*, it takes only an adverbial phrase, "comme par hasard", on the practical level of historical events, to suggest the doubt and the direction and another adverbial phrase, *le hasard* "en apparence", to imply truth on the spiritual level. "Le mot de Galilée que la foule des Juifs prononça comme par hasard en accusant J.-C. devant Pilate donne sujet à Pilate d'envoyer J.-C. à Hérode. En quoi fut accompli le mystère qu'il devait être jugé par les Juifs et les Gentils. Le hasard en apparence fut la cause de l'accomplissement du mystère" (550).

If chance in all its disguises needs to have the cloak of illusion torn from it, is chance, which seemed an observable phenomenon and a fact—is chance itself only appearance and illusion? Pascal comes back to his original questions, always considered from the point of view of infinity. The prophecies of the Old Testament become in a sense a *figure*: "Et ce qui couronne tout cela est la prédiction afin qu'on ne dît point que c'est le hasard qui l'a fait" (326). Since our limitation and distortions blind us, we must see this as actors in a specific situation: "Quiconque n'ayant plus que 8 jours à vivre ne trouvera pas que le parti est de croire que tout cela n'est pas un coup de hasard." Our vision must be other than this: "Or si les passions ne nous tenaient point, 8 jours et cent ans sont une même chose" (326).

At the same time, does the cycle of doubt and discovery have its own quality of infinity? Should we say that chance, on the spiritual level, took on the cloak of predestination? The question of appearances presents itself, with its seeming disproportion: "J.-C. en la croix, entre deux larrons. Il prédit le salut à l'un et la mort à l'autre sur les mêmes apparences" (570). That, for Pascal, predestination, indeed, became only appearance seems clear from his eventual contradiction: "Les figures de la totalité de la rédemption, comme que le soleil éclaire à tous, ne marquent qu'une totalité . . . " (910) and "J.-C. rédempteur de tous" (911). Or again: "J.-C. n'a jamais condamné sans ouïr" (549). The purpose is constructive and the movement is forward: "Quand on dit que J.-C. n'est pas mort pour tous, vous abusez d'un vice des hommes qui s'appliquent incontinent cette exception, ce qui est favoriser le désespoir au lieu de les en détourner pour favoriser l'espérance" (912). It is only on this level, and with this assurance, that the comic approach has been abandoned in the *Pensées*, marked in the midst of this very sentence by the shift from the impersonal "on" to a separation of himself from the thought expressed and a direct attack in the pronoun "vous".

Humor Applied to Specific Areas: Medicine and Law, Education, Art

Medicine and law.

Helplessness before the practitioners of medicine is a situation which invites comedy in the minds of many great writers. Second only to the medical men are the representatives of the law for their power to inspire frustration and ridicule.

It is impossible not to appreciate the droll, very human sketch of the magistrate listening to a sermon: "Que le prédicateur vienne à paraître, si la nature lui (a) donné une voix enrouée et un tour de visage bizarre, que son barbier l'ait mal rasé, si le hasard l'a encore barbouillé de surcroît, quelque grandes vérités qu'il annonce je parie la perte de la gravité de notre sénateur" (44). In ridiculing the lawmaker, Pascal has managed to burlesque the preacher.

Again, in one thrust Pascal disposes of men in law and medicine. The comic elements he uses are rich, dense in their interweaving, picturesque, effective, and remain light and elegant in the synthesis. He chooses his comic situations and characters with judgment as sure and deft as Molière's or La Fontaine's. Pascal begins with an appearance of admiration: "Nos magistrats ont

148

bien connu ce mystère [the power of imagination over reason]" (44). A scene follows, as vivid as a fable of La Fontaine. This is accomplished by various means: the picturesqueness of color, material, design and detail; the touch of raillery through metaphor in the verb "s'emmaillotent"; the caricature in the choice of the items of costume;[1] the description building, in the structure of the sentence, toward the verb; the old Gallic theme of the *dupeur* in the main verb. All this goes into one delightful sentence: "Leurs robes rouges, leurs hermines, dont ils s'emmaillotent en chaffourés, les palais où ils jugent les fleurs de lys, tout cet appareil auguste était fort nécessaire, et si les médecins n'avaient des soutanes et des mules, et que les docteurs n'eussent des bonnets carrés et des robes trop amples de quatre parties, jamais ils n'auraient dupé le monde qui ne peut résister à cette montre si authentique" (44). His characters sweep along and caper in their false dignity.

Even the direct conclusion, like a moral for the fable, builds to climax in the mask of comedy: "S'ils avaient la véritable justice, et si les médecins avaient le vrai art de guérir ils n'auraient que faire de bonnets carrés [truth in abstract terms; appearance, in a concrete picture, of one article of dress, using the superficial, recognizable detail for the caricature]. La majesté de ces sciences serait assez vénérable d'elle-même, mais n'ayant que des sciences imaginaires il faut qu'ils prennent ces vains instruments. . . . Ils s'établissent . . . par grimace" (44). The terms for appearances are clear: "des sciences imaginaires", "ces vains instruments", *"masqués*

1. M. Chevalier's reading implies comparison with an animal, "en chats fourrés"—Pléiade ed., 104—(which makes one think further of La Fontaine, and allegory), and he has the copy, Fonds français, BN 9303, to uphold it, "dont ils s'emmaillotent en chats fourrez", but this is crossed out. M. Lafuma reads: "en chaffourés". The ms. shows: "eng chafoures".

d'habits extraordinaires pour *paraître* tels [the italics are not Pascal's]" (44). With the old theme of comedy, *le dupeur dupé*, at its most profoundly symbolic level, one is not only prone to being duped by the charlatan, but one dupes oneself by the power of imagination. The use of comedy as the mask of truth is further transposed to a supernatural level. Imagination takes on a diabolical beauty: "L'imagination dispose de tout; elle fait la beauté, la justice et le bonheur qui est le tout du monde." Yet it is directed and used by a higher Power: "cette faculté trompeuse qui semble nous être donnée exprès pour nour induire à une erreur nécessaire" (44). The negative and the positive are faces of truth.

The vast fresco of the human condition unfolds, which other authors have envisaged under such titles as *la Comédie humaine* or the *Divine Comedy.*

Education.

Education becomes comic in that it prepares deliberately for "appearances"; and, inversely, man is proud of what he is not. The ideal of an *honnête homme* has its universal aspect as well as its specific seventeenth-century application. Pascal meditates thus on his immediate society: "On n'apprend point aux hommes à être honnestes hommes, et on leur apprend tout le reste. Et ils ne se piquent jamais tant de savoir rien du reste comme d'être honnestes hommes. Ils ne se piquent de savoir que la seule chose qu'ils n'apprennent point" (778). Yet the ironic contradiction itself implies the existence of the ideal in the human mind.

As always with Pascal, such ideas move with elaboration of the concrete and the greatest possible depth and height of the ideal. The word "divertissement" comes back to its original meaning of getting off the track in the caricature of the busy man (educated, futilely, to his busyness) of the seventeenth or of the twentieth century, since he is all men: "Divertissement. On charge les hommes dès l'enfance du soin de leur honneur, de leur bien, de leurs amis, et encore du bien et de l'honneur de leurs amis, on les accable d'affaires, de l'apprentissage des langues et d'exercices, et on leur fait entendre qu'ils ne sauraient être heureux, sans que leur santé, leur honneur, leur fortune, et celles de leurs amis soient en bon état, et qu'une seule chose qui manque les rendra malheureux!" (139). Appearance which immediately implies the contradiction in truth brings out the comedy with the statement, "Voilà direz-vous une étrange manière de les rendre heureux", and the question, "que pourrait-on faire de mieux pour les rendre malheureux?" Has it been far from the experience of the modern "business" man to reflect ruefully as an afterthought (as Pascal added in the margin—BN 9203), "Que le coeur de l'homme est creux & pleine [sic] d'ordure"?

For the truth is approached, and seeming reality becomes comedy from the point of view of infinity, with the axis of the three questions that sketch the human being's horizons and universe: "Comment! ce qu'on pourrait faire: il ne faudrait que leur ôter tous ces soucis, car alors ils se verraient, ils penseraient à ce qu'ils sont, d'où ils viennent, où ils vont. . . . " The comic mask implies the ideal, *le Dieu caché*. With our limited and distorted human vision we must see truth through illusion. In the same sentence Pascal reverts to the disproportion: "et ainsi on ne peut trop les occuper et les détourner." He places this deliberate "education" on the same level as diversion: "Et c'est pourquoi, après leur avoir tant préparé d'affaires, s'ils ont quelque temps de relâche, on leur conseille de l'employer à se divertir, et jouer, et s'occuper toujours tout entiers" (139). The profound question remains for us concerning the proper use of leisure (to find direction and justification for action?).

Art in writing, painting, music, dancing.

Preoccupation with art Pascal classifies as diversion, though it is not to be assumed that he lacked appreciation of art. He chooses lofty examples: "Homère fait un roman. . . . Il ne pensait pas aussi à en faire une histoire, mais seulement un divertissement . . . " (436). He says of Plato and Aristotle: "quand ils se sont divertis à faire leurs lois et leurs politiques ils l'ont fait en se jouant." Beauty remains a positive value: "l'Iliade . . . la beauté de l'ouvrage fait durer la chose" (436).

Pascal is not one to agonize, like Mallarmé, at the futility the artist may experience in his attempt to express his vision; he takes a detached view of a writer's points of frustration. His humorous observation on the upside-down quality of a human's approach to writing produces a dynamic principle of order: "La dernière chose qu'on trouve en faisant un ouvrage est de savoir celle qu'il faut mettre la première" (976). The unexpected gives fresh perspective; the quickness and subtlety of wit is the springboard for thought. If the conclusion first conceived becomes the introduction of a work, creative thought will carry farther in height and depth.

He meditates on form and order and seems to smile at curious conclusions as at delightful surprises. It is like a game in which the medium of which one disposes plays a trick on the artist. In this consideration of the effect of form, one thinks of Valéry in *Eupalinos* and the question and answer in the process of artistic creation. But Pascal's tone indicates diversion. Thus, "les mêmes mots forment d'autres pensées par leur différente disposition" (696); and, "Un même sens change selon les

paroles qui l'expriment. Les sens reçoivent des paroles
leur dignité au lieu de la leur donner" (789). It is as
though the creator, even though he chooses the words,
were to some degree the victim of them.

His tone is light when he parries a supposed critic's
thrust: "Qu'on ne dise pas que je n'ai rien dit de nouveau,
la disposition des matières est nouvelle." His example
comes from a game, a sport: "Quand on joue à la paume
c'est une même balle dont joue l'un et l'autre, mais l'un
la place mieux" (696). It is a bantering: "I won that
round."

Words have other tricks to play on poor humans. He
uncovers the unconscious betrayal of self in the words
one uses, particularly poking fun at puffed up condescension and disparagement: "Nul ne dit courtisan
que ceux qui ne le sont pas, pédant, qu'un pédant, provincial, qu' (un) provincial, et je gagerais [another game]
que c'est l'imprimeur qui l'a mis au titre des *lettres au
provincial*" (888).

He mocks the "précieux" in language, as Molière did
his *précieuses ridicules* or Alceste the pretentious and
empty poetry of Oronte. He attacks in terms of "mask"
and "disguise": "Masquer la nature et la déguiser. Plus
de roi, de pape, d'évêque, mais auguste monarque, etc.,
point de Paris, capitale du royaume. Il y a des lieux où
il faut appeler Paris, Paris, et d'autres où il la faut
appeler capitale du royaume" (509). It would be a
pleasure to have heard Pascal speak that thought,
doubtless with as much verve and gesture as Alceste
pricking the balloon of Oronte's pride.

He infers that the writer can be carried away by technique: "Eloquence. Il faut de l'agréable et du réel, mais
il faut que cet agréable soit (aussi réel) lui-même pris
du vrai" (667). The variant he crossed out.

He disparages the writer who does not know when to

stop; the superfluous is the mark of the would-be artist who is only an artisan. "L'éloquence est une peinture de la pensée, et ainsi ceux qui après avoir peint ajoutent encore font un tableau au lieu d'un portrait" (578).

He has looked carefully, and a bit cynically, at paintings and does not swallow easily the basic principle of symmetry: "Symétrie. en ce qu'on voit d'une vue. fondée sur ce qu'il n'y a pas de raison de faire autrement." His view widens to encompass the limitations of poor humans: "Et fondée aussi sur la figure de l'homme. D'où il arrive qu'on ne veut la symétrie qu'en largeur, non en hauteur, ni profondeur" (580). Painting is one more expression of the human comedy. The comic technique of the *Pensées* is a spiritual movement, upsetting symmetry at every level.

Music, by its very order, causes him to reflect on human disorder. The metaphor of music is used for disparagement, for ironic diminution, in the *pensée* classified under "Misère" (*IIIe liasse*). Yet a majestic instrument of great range and subtlety furnishes the image for the study of human nature. "Inconstance. On croit toucher des orgues ordinaries en touchant l'homme. Ce sont des orgues à la vérité, mais bizarres, changeantes, variables. . . . (Ceux qui ne savent toucher que les ordinaires) ne feraient pas d'accords[2] sur celles-là. Il faut savoir où sont les (touches)" (55). He stressed the lack of predictable order in the human, having noted the sweetly graded movement in line of the usual organ pipes, in the words he suppressed after "variables": "dont les tuyaux ne se suivent pas par degrés conjoints." The lute is designated as unworthy distraction with its elusive and too delicate charm: "Or à quoi pense le monde? . . . à jouer du luth" (620). Note, however,

_____

2. M. Lafuma reads: "ne seraient pas d'accord_". The ms. seems clearly to read: "ne *f*eraient pas d'accords", as the Pléiade edition has it.

Pascal's appreciation of this gentle instrument: "Raison des effets. La faiblesse de l'homme est la cause de tant de beautés qu'on établit, comme de savoir bien jouer du luth n'est un mal qu'à cause de notre faiblesse" (96). Even great harmony in music does not strike an answering chord in pitiable humans, "Bornés en tout genre": "trop de consonances déplaisent dans la musique" (199). Music here points up the "Disproportion de l'homme" and serves (*XVe liasse.* "Transition.") as an element of transition between the senses and a spiritual concept: "Nous brûlons du désir de trouver . . . une tour qui s'élève à (l') infini" (199). Irony serves to affirm the infinite through the realization of "l'inconstance des apparences" (199).

Surely Pascal must have tried dancing. References creep in. Dancing remains a symbol of pure diversion, dangerous by its attraction, classed with gaming and with theater. The comic position of the human is intense and misplaced absorption. It is in the group of *pensées* on the subject of the king left without diversion that Pascal suppressed this sentence: "L'unique bien des hommes consiste donc à être divertis de penser à leur condition ou par une occupation qui les en détourne, ou par quelque passion agréable et nouvelle qui les occupe, ou par le jeu, la chasse, quelque spectacle attachant, et enfin par ce qu'on appelle divertissement" (136). One notes the confusion in his mind of these two prime examples of diversion. In the manuscript he wrote first *la danse*, crossed out *danse* and wrote *chasse*.

He was aware of the absorbing quality of dancing, having added in the left margin:[3] "La danse, yl [ms.] faut bien penser où l'on mettra ses pieds" (136).[4] One

3. *Le manuscrit des* Pensées *de Pascal, 1662.* ed. Louis Lafuma, p. 71.
4. Molière does not neglect the comic possibilities of the dancing master in *le Bourgeois gentilhomme.*

visualizes the frustration and awkwardness of the beginner in dancing. Dancing is linked with hunting: "Le gentilhomme croit sincèrement que la chasse est . . . un plaisir royal" (136); and in speaking of "la dignité royale", he concedes ironically: "Je vois bien que c'est rendre un homme heureux de le divertir de la veue [ms.] de ses misères domestiques pour remplir toutes ses pensées du soin de bien danser . . . " (137).

Pascal gives us a phrase which carries the rhythm of the music (the explosive consonants have the force of onomatopoeia, set the mincing rhythm of the dance, and call forth a smile): "occuper son âme à penser à ajuster ses pas à la cadence d'un air" (137), on a level with deftness in athletics, "ou à placer adroitement une barre" (137). In another passage (unclassified, and crossed out, possibly because it was condensed and incorporated into *pensée* 136,[5] such activity suggested to him the absorption of competition, and the word used is the same as for the hunt: "On vient du lui [servir] une balle et il faut qu'il la rejette à son compagnon. Il est occupé à la prendre à la chute du toit pour gagner une chasse" (522).

Through these variants, additions, suppressions, there takes place a generalization along with the concrete image of the king. In the dramatic tradition of classicism, Pascal chooses the most illustrious personage for his central character. Generalized, the thought has to do with "les hommes" and their deliberate schooling for these pursuits: "Divertissement. On charge les hommes, dès l'enfance . . . " (139).

The human being is the comic character. The search for pleasure drives the man; the aberration has taken over. He is not his own man: "ils recherchent . . . une

5. "la moindre chose comme un billard et une balle qu'il pousse, suffisent pour le divertir" (136).

occupation violente et impétueuse. . . . ils se proposent
un objet attirant qui les charme et les attire avec ardeur
. . . " (137).

Man is the king, and the king is man. The thought is
clear in the passage: "On vient de lui [servir] une balle.
. . . " The appreciation of adept absorption leads to a
satirical sentence, castigating, righteously indignant,
which lifts the image to a spiritual level. Man is the
king, dethroned but royal, and required to recognize
his royalty: "Voilà un soin digne d'occuper cette grande
âme, et de lui ôter toute autre pensée de l'esprit. Cet
homme né pour connaître l'univers, pour juger de toutes
choses, pour régir tout un Etat, le voilà occupé et tout
rempli du [soin] de prendre un lièvre. Et s'il ne s'abaisse
à cela et veuille toujours être tendu [*occupé*, crossed
out] il n'en sera que plus sot, parce qu'il voudra s'élever
au-dessus de l'hu[manité] et il n'est qu'un homme au
bout [du compte] c'est-à-dire capable de peu et [de
beaucoup] de tout et de rien; il n'est ne [ange] ni bête
mais homme" (522). The balanced cadence of the last
half of the sentence, "et il n'est qu'un homme . . . ", con-
trols and disciplines the violence of satire and restores
the tone of respect and courtesy in the conclusion, "mais
homme".

The thought and image interlaced are clear in the
passage which transposes the "order" important in
art to order in thought on the spiritual plane: " . . .
l'ordre de la pensée est de commercer par soi, et par
son auteur et sa fin" (620). The ridicule is in the question: "Or à quoi pense le monde? jamais à cela, mais
à danser, à jouer du luth, à chanter, à faire des vers, à
courir la bague etc. et à se battre, à se faire roi, sans
penser à ce que c'est qu'être roi et qu'être homme" (620).
The synthesis comes even clearer: "Toutes ces misères-là
même prouvent sa grandeur. Ce sont misères de grand

seigneur. Misères d'un roi dépossédé" (116), and: "La grandeur de l'homme . . . se tire de sa misère . . . il est déchu d'une meilleure nature qui lui était propre autrefois. Car qui se trouve malheureux de n'être pas roi sinon un roi dépossédé" (117). Voltaire in *Candide* recognized the comedy in the situation of dispossessed kings. Pascal sees as clearly their ludicrous position, but the comedy takes on the depth of symbol.

And "la chasse", whether in sportive competition or in the royal occupation of the hunt, becomes "la recherche": "Ils ne savent pas que ce n'est que la chasse et non la prise qu'ils recherchent" (136). This absorption becomes a "figure", an image. It leads to contradiction in the speculation that "ils ont un autre instinct secret qui reste de la grandeur de notre première nature, qui leur fait connaître que le bonheur n'est en effet que dans le repos, et non pas dans le tumulte" (136). The variant, suppressed, for "le tumulte" is "la recherche".[6] The movement of *la recherche* continues, for: "Notre nature est dans le mouvement, le repos entier est la mort" (641). The contradiction implicit in life and death, movement and repose, at once ridicules and dignifies human pursuit of happiness.

Does art and its attraction, which remains a diversion, a distraction, an "appearance", a way for the human, *le dupeur*, to dupe himself, also prefigure "la beauté qui fait durer" on the spiritual plane, the true "joy" of the *Mémorial*? The opposite of this absorption is "l'ennui", so profoundly experienced by Baudelaire, so rhythmically contained in that modern poem that is the *pensée* entitled "Ennui": "Rien n'est si insupportable . . . " (622).[7]

6. Pléiade ed., 205.
7. Mr. Mortimer (p. 119) has noted the "strange strophic form in which it appears in Pascal's handwriting". The manuscript shows the

To destroy the attraction of appearances would allow "l'ennui" to enter, efficaciously: "Misère. . . . Sans cela [le divertissement], nous serions dans l'ennui, et cet ennui nous pousserait à chercher un moyen plus solide d'en sortir, mais le divertissement nous amuse et nous fait arriver insensiblement à la mort" (414).

This is the true function of humor, the detachment that sees distortion and contradiction (diversion and boredom alike) as "appearance", and has the courage to laugh, preliminary to the step in faith which is spiritual advancement.

---

lines divided thus: Ennui. Rien n'est si insupportable / à l'homme que d'être / dans un plein repos, / sans passions, sans affaire, / sans divertissement, sans application. / Il sent alors son néant, son abandon, / son insuffisance, sa dépendance, / son impuissance, son vide [all of this sentence added at the right in the manuscript, for insertion after "application"]. Incontinent il sortira du fond de / son âme—l'ennui,—la / noirceur, la tristesse, / le chagrin, le dépit, le / désespoir. "Désespoir" stands alone as the final line (BN 9202 ms. original, f° 47).

The Symbolic Role of Comedy
in the *Pensées*

What more sobering thought for the twentieth century with its triumphant move into space than Pascal's: "Roseau pensant. Ce n'est point de l'espace que je dois chercher ma dignité, mais c'est du règlement de ma pensée. Je n'aurais pas d'avantage en possédant des terres. Par l'espace l'univers me comprend et m'engloutit comme un point: par la penseé je le comprends" (113)? What greater encouragement than the unending "recherche" of Pascal? To Gilberte he writes in the spring of 1645:[1] "Les choses corporelles ne sont qu'une image des spirituelles, et Dieu a représenté les choses invisibles dans les visibles. . . . Nous devons nous considérer comme des criminelles dans une prison toute remplie des images de leur libérateur et des instructions nécessaires pour sortir de la servitude." Often it takes humor with its impersonal perspective and its courage to liberate ourselves from our successive prisons and to find joy in the process.

Pascal's techniques in comedy are more varied than in the *Provinciales* and more profound in their use. We have noted: the unexpected within a sentence, or in a situation, or in a figure of speech; the grotesque, the incongruous; caricature by gesture; belittling humor, irony in an adjective, or an adverb, or a verb (in the midst of an otherwise straightforward, serious sentence);

1. Mortimer, *Blaise Pascal,* p. 75.

160

irony through disproportion, or by metaphor within metaphor; dynamic and comic antithesis of the small cause and the vast result; the use of derogatory terms or names bringing characters to life in conversation; juxtaposition of the concrete and the abstract, forcing the reader to smile in the obvious attitude of common sense; onomatopoeia as effective as gesture seen on the stage; imagery, concrete and vivid, to point up unreasonableness and foolishness; true comic situations and characters, as in charlatanry in medicine; dramatic situation and crescendo in effect to light up the ridiculous (so close to the sublime); traditional comic themes, *le dupeur dupé*, raised to symbolic meaning; costume as symbol; and the tones of light raillery, teasing, gentle irony, sarcasm, bitter and violent satire.

Pascal has the enthusiasm of a Rabelais in the multiplicity of his comic effects, not for the enjoyment of technique in itself, but with great inherent discipline in the application of the process.

The density of techniques of humor in the *Pensées* represents the metaphor and paradox of human existence, a metaphor essentially comic and ridiculous. Is not the central figure of *l'Apologie, le roi dépossédé*, one who uses appearances to deceive others and oneself, the embodiment of the persistent theme of *l'esprit gaulois, le dupeur dupé*? The humorous effects are less obvious than in the *Provinciales*, more condensed, subtle, and symbolic. They are effective for being presented courteously and charitably, in that Pascal shares with all men the burden of human foolishness.

Pascal apparently did not regret the violence of his attack in the *Provinciales*. M. Steinmann notes that in 1662 Pascal affirmed that if he had them to do over again, he would make them even stronger.[2] Neverthe-

2. Steinmann, *Pascal*, p. 123, and his edition of *les Provinciales*

less, he abandoned the work for greater objectivity, for higher comic art, designed to lead and persuade and recreate all men, not to destroy a few. In the impersonality of comic vision on a cosmic level Pascal finds his greatest artistic strength. By clever, graceful, sudden inversions of thought and language intended to please and delight and disturb, the delicacy and lightness of comedy is redeemed and made constructive by the eminently serious import of his greatest work. His aim then remains the aim of all great art, to elevate and ennoble the human spirit. Comedy, well-used, is essential in the classic attitude.

(Paris: Colin, 1962), p. 12. M. Béguin attributes the leaving of the work unfinished to another reason: "cette mobile impatience qui le détourne d'une étude dès qu'il a appréhendé les premiers principes"—Albert Béguin, *Pascal par lui-même* (Paris: Seuil, 1958), p. 5.

Bibliography of Works Cited

Alcorn, John M. "Sight and Satire; the Quality of Vision in the Writings of Molière, Pascal, and Swift." Deposited Harvard University Library, June 18, 1951.

Baudelaire, Charles. *Oeuvres complètes*, Bibliothèque de la Pléiade. Paris: Gallimard, 1961.

Baudouin, Charles. *Blaise Pascal ou l'ordre du coeur.* Paris: Plon, 1962.

Béguin, Albert. *Pascal par lui-même.* Paris: Seuil, 1958.

Bergson, Henri. *Oeuvres.* Paris: Presses Universitaires de France, 1959.

Carnochan, W. B. "Juvenal as a Satirist." *PMLA*, March, 1970.

Chestov, Leo. *In Job's Balances. On the Sources of the Eternal Truths.* London: J. M. Dent & Sons, 1932.

Demorest, Jean-Jacques. "Pascal et le déséquilibre." *PMLA*, May, 1967.

Diéguez, Manuel de. *Essai sur l'avenir poétique de Dieu. Bossuet, Pascal, Chateaubriand, Claudel.* Paris: Plon, 1965.

Einstein, Albert. "Only Then Shall We Find Courage." Reprinted from the *New York Times Magazine.* Pamphlet issued by the Emergency Committee of Atomic Scientists, 21 May, 1947.

Exposition, "Deux siècles de Jansénisme à travers les documents du fonds Port-Royal d'Utrecht," Musée de l'Histoire de France, 16 janvier - 18 mars 1974.

163

Fontenelle, Bernard Le Bovier de. *Oeuvres complètes.* Genève: Slatkine Reprints, 1968. Réimpression de l'édition de Paris, 1818.

Fromm, Erich. *The Art of Loving.* New York: Harper & Row, 1956. New York: Bantam Books, 1963.

Green, Julien. *Vers l'invisible (1958-1967).* Paris: Plon, 1967.

Guardini, Romano. *Pascal for Our Time,* tr. Brian Thompson. New York: Herder and Herder, 1966.

Guillemin, Henri. *L'Humour de Victor Hugo.* Neuchatel: Ed. de la Baconnière, 1951.

Guitton, Jean. *Génie de Pascal.* Paris: Aubier, 1962.

Jerphagnon, Lucien. *Le Caractère de Pascal. Essai de caractérologie littéraire.* Paris: Presses Universitaires de France, 1962.

Lafuma, Louis. *Histoire des* Pensées *de Pascal (1656-1952).* Paris: Nizet, 1969.

Le Moine, Pierre. *La Dévotion aisée,* par le jésuite Pierre le Moine, 1652.

Mortimer, Ernest. *Blaise Pascal, the Life and Work of a Realist.* London: Methuen, 1959.

Pascal, Blaise. *Oeuvres complètes.* Les Grands Ecrivains de la France. Ed. L. Brunschvig, P. Boutroux, and F. Gazier. Paris: Hachette, 1914-1923.

———. *Oeuvres complètes,* Bibliothèque de la Pléaide. Paris: Gallimard, 1954.

———. *Oeuvres complètes,* l'Intégrale. Paris: Seuil, 1963.

———. *Le manuscrit des* Pensées *de Pascal, 1662.* Ed. Louis Lafuma. Paris: Les Libraires Associés, 1962.

———. *Les Pensées.* Original manuscript. Bibliothèque Nationale. B. N. Fonds français, ms. 9202.

———. *Les Pensées.* Copy of the manuscript. Bibliothèque

Nationale. B. N. Fonds français, ms. 9203.

———. *Les Pensées*. Ed. Louis Lafuma. Paris: Seuil, 1962.

——— . *Les Provinciales*. Ed. Jean Steinmann. Paris: Colin, 1962.

Racine, Jean. *Oeuvres complètes*. Paris: Seuil, 1962.

Sainte-Beuve. *Pascal et Port-Royal*. In Pascal, *Les Provinciales*. Paris: Nouvel Office d'Edition, 1964.

Slights, William W. E. "Pattern and *Persona* in Pascal's *Lettres provinciales*." *Kentucky Romance Quarterly* 14 (1967), 126-138.

Steinmann, Jean. *Pascal*. Paris: Desclée de Brouwer, 1962.

Strowski, Fortunat. *Pascal et son temps. Histoire du sentiment religieux en France au XVIIe siècle*, III, *Les Provinciales et Les Pensées*. Paris: Plon, 1928.

Weber, Joseph Gardner. "Person as Figure of Ambiguity and Resolution in Pascal." *PMLA*, vol. 84, no. 2 (March, 1969).

———. "The Persuasive Art of Pascal's *Lettres Provinciales*: A Study of Satire, Irony and Argumentation." Ph. D. dissertation, Illinois University, 1963.

Wells, Albert N. *Pascal's Recovery of Man's Wholeness*. Richmond, Va.: John Knox, 1965.

Zwillenberg, Myrna Kogan. "Dramatic Justice in *Tartuffe*." *Modern Language Notes* (May, 1975), 583-590.